Public Health Entrepreneurship
Navigating the Intersection of Purpose and Profit

Quisha Umemba, MPH, BSN, RN, CDCES, CHWI
Visionary Author

Co-Authored By:
Dr. Jovonni Spinner, Jometra Hawkins, Vanessa Da Costa

Copyright © 2024 by Quisha Umemba.

All Rights Reserved. No part of this publication may be reproduced, distributed, or transmitted in any form or by any means, including photocopying, recording, or other electronic or mechanical methods, without the prior written permission of the publisher or author(s), except in the case of brief quotations embodied in critical reviews and certain other non-commercial uses permitted by copyright law.

ISBN: 979-8-9876649-7-1
Edited, Formatted and Published by Empower Her Publishing, LLC in Richmond, VA.

www.empowerherpublishing.com.

Printed in the United States of America.

The information in this book is intended solely for educational and informational purposes. It is not intended as professional or legal advice. The author and publisher disclaim any liability or responsibility for any errors or omissions in the content.

Trademarked names, logos, and images that may appear in this book are used for editorial purposes only and remain the property of their respective owners. There is no intention of trademark infringement.

For permission or inquiries, please contact Quisha Umemba at quisha@umembahealth.com.

Dedication

This book is dedicated to my mother, Carolyn Jean Rochelle (née Easter), who shared many valuable life lessons with me over the years. Of them all, these three lessons have impacted my life the most.

1. Never let "them" see you sweat.
2. Always walk with your head high.
3. You can be anything in the world that you want to be if you dream big and work hard.

Thank you for molding me into the woman I am today and for giving me permission to be great.

This book is also dedicated to you – the enthusiastic public health professional who so desperately wants to show up in the world in a greater capacity, create a legacy of impact, and live out your purpose and passion. I give you the same gift my mother gave me: permission to be anything you want to be if you dream big and work hard.

Preface

My Story
Growing up, I was driven by an innate desire to help others and make a meaningful impact in my community. My early experiences as a Candy Striper ignited the flames of compassion and service within me. However, life had its own plans. I married at 19 and had my first son the next year which diverged the path of my initial dream of becoming a Physician. Instead, I decided to pursue a certification in Medical Assisting (MA).

After graduating as Valedictorian in the MA program, it was the gentle encouragement from one of my instructors that suggested I go to nursing school, so I did. For me, nursing was more than just a profession; it was my calling. But, a few years into my nursing career, I started to notice a trend. Patients would come to the hospital in an acute state for a chronic condition, spend a few days, a few weeks, or sometimes a few months, then get discharged only to return several days, several weeks, or sometimes several months later in a worse condition than they were during the previous hospitalization. I noticed that despite the education and care I provided or the dedication that I poured into nursing my patients back to health, this challenge persisted. In fact, it often felt like a revolving door, with patients returning to the hospital, their health conditions seemingly impervious to my efforts.

Then I was introduced to public health. A windshield assessment assignment in a community nursing class opened my eyes to the social determinants of health (SDoH), the conditions people live in which often affect health outcomes, and the critical role they play in shaping an individual's well-being. This revelation led me to pursue a Master of Public Health (MPH) degree with a focus on health education and human behavior. Armed with a new mission, I sought out to better understand the drivers that contribute to poor health outcomes in individuals and communities and pluck them at the root. This would be my new profession, but it would also be my new calling.

After grad school, I landed my first public health role as a Chief Nurse in the third largest local health department (LHD) in the United States. I worked there for four years before landing my second role in public health as a Diabetes Nurse Consultant with a state health department. In these positions, I witnessed firsthand the profound impact of (SDoH) on health outcomes and the potential for change through innovative health promotion programming and community-based partnerships and collaborations. I loved the work I did at the local and state levels of public health, but the work wasn't without its challenges. The rigid structures of traditional public health and the labyrinthine bureaucracy often hindered the swift and effective responses needed to address the pressing health disparities in the communities I served. I grew frustrated with the slow pace of decision-making and the constraints imposed by traditional funding sources. In my quest for more responsive and impactful solutions, I ventured (eyes wide open) into entrepreneurship. In 2019, and while still working full-time, I incorporated Umemba Health LLC, a public health consultancy committed to transforming the field of public health through comprehensive workforce development.

Why I Wrote This Book
I wrote this book for several reasons. First, to share my personal journey to entrepreneurship and how my experiences as a nurse and public health practitioner have shaped my perspective and influenced my path to business ownership. I wrote this book because of the passion I have for public health in general. As *"the nurse who got bitten by the public health bug"*, I discovered that the fervor I once had for bedside care expanded exponentially when I shifted my focus from individuals to entire communities. Now zip codes, cities, and states have become my patients and I have grown to love and care for them in the same way I cared for my patients in the hospitals and clinics where I worked as a nurse.

Secondly, I wrote this book to fill a gap when I noticed the lack of existing literature and resources related to public health entrepreneurship. As a matter of fact, there have been so few articles and books written on the topic, I completed my literature review in a weekend. At the time of the writing of this book, not one book had been published on the topic of public health entrepreneurship, aside from my eBook: An Introduction to Entrepreneurship for Public Health Professionals.

Lastly, my motivation for writing this book stems from the profound impact I hope it will have on the public health community at large and to inspire and empower both public health professionals and aspiring entrepreneurs. The wisdom shared within these pages is not only intended to impart knowledge but also to offer actionable steps and strategies that readers can readily apply as they embark on their own public health entrepreneurial journey.

Within the pages of this book, I will discuss the role and impact of public health and why traditional public health needs a revolution. I will share inspiring stories and impactful contributions of everyday individuals driving innovation in the field as public health consultants and entrepreneurs so you know you can do it too. Then I will offer practical guidance on how to leverage your expertise, package your genius, and monetize your skillset to start, grow, and scale a profitable public health consulting business that makes impact and income.

I hope that this book will become a valuable resource, guiding readers through the intricate intersection of purpose and profit successfully. It is my desire that public health professionals, who frequently grapple with the burdens of excessive workloads and insufficient compensation, will discover through these pages that they, too, possess the capacity to challenge the status quo and break free from convention to become unconventional agents of change, creating meaningful and lasting impact.

Why I'm Qualified to Write This Book
You might be wondering what qualifies me to be the author of this book and to guide you on this journey. Allow me to share my qualifications:

- *I possess a multi-faceted expertise*: With 20+ years of diverse experience as a Registered Nurse, Public Health Expert, and now Entrepreneur, my expertise spans both the healthcare and public health fields. I have worked in inpatient, outpatient, and in community settings, a federal agency, in state and local government, and in Corporate America. This real-world experience has equipped me with insights into the challenges and opportunities that public health professionals and organizations encounter daily.

- *I am a public health entrepreneur:* Within the confines of this book, I share information that comes from firsthand experience as a full-time self-employed public health consultant and entrepreneur. I'm not just telling you what I heard or witnessed. I'm not just sharing stories of other successful entrepreneurs. I'm sharing what I know and what I know to be true of public health entrepreneurship.

- *A proven track record of success*: After two and a half years of "side hustling" and within four years total, I have built a multi-six-figure public health workforce development business that has trained over 3,000 public health professionals representing more than 300 organizations. This is a significant impact for a small organization and it showcases my ability to develop and deliver educational content tailored to the needs of public health professionals. That's why I now coach other public health professionals using my proprietary step-by-step systems and strategies that have been proven to yield success when it comes to starting, building, and launching a public health consulting business.

As you delve into the pages that follow, you will find that my qualifications go beyond academic degrees and professional titles (although I have those too). You will see that I stand firmly in my belief that public health professionals are best suited to lead the way in public health innovation and that I encompass a deep commitment and a genuine desire to help them do so.

How This Book Will Benefit You
This book is the culmination of my experiences, successes, and the blueprint I've developed to help others embark on the entrepreneurial journey and be successful. As you read the chapters that follow, you'll learn to bridge the gap between purpose and profit and how to address pressing public health issues while also building a profitable and sustainable business venture. Each chapter is designed to provide you with valuable insights, actionable steps, and the knowledge to navigate the complexities of this exhilarating journey.

Consider this book your call to action! However, it will only serve you if you actively engage with the content and apply the principles discussed in the book. This book is more than just information; it's an invitation to become a change-maker in the world of public health. It's an invitation to join me in unlocking the potential of social entrepreneurship, where passion, innovation, and purpose converge to create a healthier future for all. I hope you are ready to embrace the opportunities and possibilities that exist in public health entrepreneurship. I hope you are ready to join me on the path to purpose and profit. Let's get started!

Table of Contents

Dedication..iii

Preface..v

Part 1 - Purpose: The Pursuit of Health Equity..........1
    Chapter 1: The Role and Impact of Public Health in Society..3
    Chapter 2: Entrepreneurship in the Context of Public Health..9
    Chapter 3: My Journey into Public Health Entrepreneurship...25

Part 2 - Passion: Public Health Entrepreneurs – Profiles of Impact...37
    Chapter 4: From Scrubs to Strategy by Quisha Umemba...39
    Chapter 5: Breaking Down Barriers to Support Healthy Communities by Dr. Jovonni Spinner........61
    Chapter 6: Bridging My Life's Purpose to Profit by Jometra Hawkins..87
    Chapter 7: Taking Action Beyond Data Insights by Vanessa Da Costa.......................................103

Part 3 - Profit: The Path to a Profitable (and Sustainable) Public Health Consulting Business..........123
    Chapter 8: Starting Your Public Health Business....125
    Chapter 9: Growing Your Public Health Consulting Business..141
    Chapter 10: Scaling Your Public Health Business...163
    Chapter 11: Purpose and Profit: Balancing Your Bottom Line with Your Higher Calling..................183

Conclusion...189

References..193

Acknowledgments..197

Bonus Content...199

"If we can FALL in love with serving people, creating value, solving problems, building valuable connections, and doing work that matters, it makes us more likely that we're going to do important work." – Seth Godin

Part 1 - Purpose: The Pursuit of Health Equity

Introduction
In a quiet corner of a neighborhood, a community health center is nestled in a concrete jungle. In this place, the waiting room is never empty. The chairs are filled with people, each carrying a unique story etched into their expressions. Some wear smiles of hope, while others bear the weight of uncertainty. It's a place where health is not just a word but a promise, a promise often met with challenges and that often goes broken.

And in this quiet (but not so quiet) corner of the world, I stood, as a young nurse with big dreams of making an impact and of being a beacon of hope and health for those who walked through the clinic's doors. Until I encountered a reality both profound and perplexing. Despite the tireless hours, the heartfelt care, and the knowledge I bestowed upon my patients every day, I watched as they returned through our doors time and time again, their health struggles far from conquered. It was a humbling realization: the complexities of health often extended beyond the scope of a prescription and my nursing care plan. And as a nurse, with all the best intentions in the world, while working in a broken healthcare system, I had to admit that nursing school left me unprepared and ill-equipped to provide the level of care that the patients in my community needed. Sometime later, I discovered public health and a profound truth—a truth that I believe probably resonates with you as well; that health is not solely about doctors and medications; it's about the communities we live in, the environments that shape us, and the opportunities we have—or lack thereof— to thrive.

This newfound discovery and deeply internalized conviction led me on a mission to address the pressing health disparities that persist in our communities. It is a mission to empower

Purpose: The Pursuit of Health Equity

individuals to take control of their well-being and it is a mission to transform the way we think about health and the possibilities that lie within our reach.

As you hold this book in your hands, I want you to feel the pulse of this mission and to sense the urgency behind it. The pain of health disparities is real and it touches lives in profound ways. But here's the counterintuitive truth: within this pain lies an opportunity, a transformative power that can reshape the landscape of public health. It's a power I've witnessed firsthand and a power that I'm excited to share with you.

In the pages that follow, you'll discover not just solutions, but a mindset—a mindset that bridges purpose and profit. You'll learn how you can be that beacon of hope and health and a beacon of change. But this journey isn't just about addressing problems; it's about envisioning a world where health disparities no longer hold sway thanks to innovative solutions. A world where communities thrive, where individuals are equipped with the tools they need to live healthy lives, and where public health professionals are revered.

I'm Quisha Umemba, The PublicHealthPreneur™, and I've dedicated my career to the pursuit of health equity, to transforming communities, and to empowering public health professionals through public health entrepreneurship. My journey is a testament to the potential of this field and my goal is to ignite that potential within you.

Chapter 1:
The Role and Impact of Public Health in Society

Defining Public Health
Public health is the science of protecting and improving the health of people and their communities (CDC Foundation, 2024). It encompasses a wide range of activities aimed at improving the health of populations, including disease surveillance, health education, policy development, and environmental interventions, just to name a few. At its core, public health seeks to prevent disease, promote health, and prolong life among communities, rather than focusing solely on individual healthcare needs. While individual healthcare focuses on diagnosing and treating illness in individual patients, public health takes a broader perspective by addressing health issues at the population level. While healthcare is reactive, responding to the health needs of individuals as they arise, public health is proactive, seeking to prevent health problems before they occur. While healthcare primarily occurs within clinical settings, public health interventions may take place in various settings, including schools, workplaces, and other community environments. Public health takes place where people live, work, learn, play, pray, and age.

The Mission of Public Health
The fundamental mission of public health is to enhance the well-being of entire populations through the mitigation of health inequities. Health inequities represent systematic disparities in health outcomes among various demographic groups, bearing substantial social and economic repercussions for both individuals and societies (World Health Organization, 2018). Reducing health disparities helps to advance health equity. Health equity is the attainment of the highest level of health for all people, where everyone has a

fair and just opportunity to attain their optimal health regardless of race, ethnicity, disability, sexual orientation, gender identity, socioeconomic status, geography, preferred language, or other factors (Centers for Medicaid and Medicare, 2023). Achieving health equity entails that every individual engaging with a healthcare system receives the necessary support to achieve optimal health outcomes. By addressing the underlying determinants of health, the social, economic, and environmental factors, public health seeks to create conditions that enable all individuals to lead healthy lives.

Public health practice is guided by several fundamental principles, including:
- *The principle of prevention.* Public health emphasizes preventing disease and injury before they occur, rather than waiting to treat them once they arise. Prevention efforts aim to reduce the occurrence of disease and injury by addressing risk factors and promoting healthy behaviors.

- *The principle of equity.* Public health seeks to achieve health equity by addressing disparities in health outcomes and ensuring that all individuals can attain their highest level of health. Achieving health equity requires concerted efforts on multiple fronts including people, processes, and policies.

- *The principle of community engagement.* Public health recognizes the importance of engaging communities in the design, implementation, and evaluation of health interventions, as community involvement enhances the effectiveness and sustainability of public health efforts.

The Impact of Public Health on Society
Public health interventions have led to significant improvements in health outcomes and quality of life across the globe. For example, vaccination programs have eradicated

deadly diseases such as smallpox and drastically reduced the incidence of polio, measles, and other infectious diseases. Sanitation measures, such as clean water systems and sewage treatment, have reduced the spread of waterborne illnesses and improved overall hygiene. Health education campaigns have raised awareness about the importance of healthy lifestyles, leading to reductions in smoking rates, increased physical activity, and improved nutrition. These examples highlight the tangible benefits of public health efforts in saving lives, preventing disease, and promoting well-being.

Public health initiatives also have far-reaching economic, social, and cultural implications for society. Economically, investments in public health yield substantial returns by reducing healthcare costs, increasing productivity, and stimulating economic growth. For instance, those same vaccination programs that have eradicated deadly diseases have also saved billions of dollars in healthcare expenses by preventing illness and reducing the need for medical treatment. Studies have shown that every $1 invested in childhood immunizations yields up to $44 in economic benefits (Ozawa et al., 2016), demonstrating the cost-effectiveness of vaccination programs. In the realm of sanitation, access to clean water and adequate sanitation facilities has been linked to reductions in diarrheal diseases and improvements in child survival rates in developing countries (Merid et al., 2023). Furthermore, health education campaigns, such as anti-smoking initiatives, have contributed to declines in smoking prevalence and improvements in public health outcomes (Golechha, 2016). Socially, public health efforts contribute to the creation of healthier and more resilient communities, fostering social cohesion and solidarity. Culturally, public health initiatives have (and can) shape societal norms and values around health, influencing behaviors, beliefs, and attitudes toward health and illness.

The Urgency of Public Health
The urgency of addressing health disparities cannot be overstated, as they not only undermine individual health but also contribute to broader societal inequities. Disparities in

health outcomes result in unnecessary suffering, premature death, and diminished quality of life for affected individuals and communities. Furthermore, these disparities impose significant economic burdens on healthcare systems, businesses, and society as a whole, as the costs of treating preventable diseases and addressing health disparities continue to escalate.

When it comes to the public health workforce, the state of urgency is equally critical. Two years of COVID response have contributed to increased stress and burnout, as well as post-traumatic stress symptoms, according to the Public Health Workforce Interests and Needs Survey, conducted between September 2021 and January 2022 (de Beaumont Foundation, 2022). Added to this, state and local health departments must hire a minimum of 80,000 more full-time equivalent positions — an increase of nearly 80% — to provide adequate infrastructure and a minimum package of public health services (de Beaumont Foundation, 2021). Developing a sense of urgency NOW is crucial for driving meaningful and swift change within public health organizations and systems. The creation of a sense of urgency is not a luxury but a necessity for public health transformation and it includes engaging all stakeholders, conventional and unconventional, to address the evolving landscape and dynamic nature of public health.

The Culture of Public Health
When I transitioned from a nursing culture known for "eating their young" to the public health field, I left behind a well-paying role for a sector where being overworked, underpaid, undervalued, and underappreciated is, unfortunately, all too common. Public health professionals, much like their counterparts in nursing, dedicate their lives to the well-being of others. While nursing is revered and consistently celebrated as one of the most trusted professions, public health professionals are often not recognized for their efforts. The irony lies in the fact that while nurses are hailed as "healthcare heroes", especially in times of crisis, public health

professionals remain the "unsung heroes", their work often invisible to the public eye, yet indispensable to the public's health.

Despite these challenges; passion, dedication, and a deep commitment to improving health and well-being remain the driving forces in both nursing and public health. These professions are bound by a shared mission to care for others, yet they are also united by the systemic challenges that can erode morale and hinder our ability to make a difference. However, it's within these challenges that opportunities for transformation lie. Public health professionals, just like nurses, deserve to be celebrated and appreciated, not just in times of crisis but every day for their unwavering commitment to the health of communities. While I do champion a culture where public health professionals are appreciated, supported, and acknowledged for their crucial role in enhancing health and well-being, I hold a perspective that might not be widely shared. I don't believe that public health can be transformed from the inside out. Instead, I'm convinced that change in public health will emerge from external influences, working their way inward.

21st Century Challenges call for 21st Century Solutions

As societal needs evolve and new threats emerge, public health professionals must remain vigilant, proactive, and innovative in their approaches to safeguarding the health and well-being of populations. As communities undergo demographic changes, such as population growth, aging populations, and urbanization, public health initiatives must adapt to address emerging health concerns and disparities. Contemporary challenges call for unconventional agents of change and there has never been a better time to seek the contributions of public health entrepreneurs.

Public health entrepreneurs are individuals who use their knowledge and skills to identify gaps in the current public health system, develop innovative solutions, and implement strategies for change in the pursuit of health equity. These

The Role and Impact of Public Health in Society

individuals come from diverse backgrounds and may have a wide range of expertise, including epidemiology, biostatistics, environmental health, social sciences, and policy development. Their unique perspectives and multidisciplinary approaches enable them to identify and address complex health issues from multiple angles.

Public health entrepreneurs also possess strong leadership skills, as they must effectively communicate their ideas, gain support from stakeholders, and navigate complex systems to implement their initiatives. They can form partnerships with community organizations, government agencies, and other key players to create a collective impact for the greater good. Furthermore, public health entrepreneurs are champions of equity and social justice. They recognize that health disparities exist in marginalized communities and work towards addressing these inequalities through their initiatives. They understand the importance of community empowerment, cultural competency, and diversity in achieving health equity.

Today, public health entrepreneurs are needed more than ever. With emerging threats like climate change, global pandemics, and the rise of chronic diseases, their skills and expertise are crucial in shaping effective and sustainable public health policies and interventions. They are constantly adapting to new challenges and finding innovative ways to promote health and prevent disease. In the upcoming chapter, we'll explore entrepreneurship from a public health perspective, delve into the landscape of public health consulting, and examine the pivotal role played by public health consultants.

Chapter 2:
Entrepreneurship in the Context of Public Health

Defining Entrepreneurship
At its most basic level, entrepreneurship refers to an individual striking out on an original path to create a new business venture. Entrepreneurship is a dynamic process of identifying opportunities, mobilizing resources, and taking calculated risks to create value in a marketplace or society. At its core, entrepreneurship involves innovation, initiative, and a willingness to challenge the status quo. This is why entrepreneurship is needed in public health. Entrepreneurship is a catalyst for innovation and transformation and can empower individuals to address societal challenges to create positive change. By embracing innovation, public health professionals can unlock new opportunities, drive sustainable progress, and advance the goal of health equity for all. The core elements of entrepreneurship include:

- *Opportunity Recognition:* Entrepreneurship begins with the identification of opportunities, whether it's spotting unmet needs, emerging trends, or gaps in the market.

- *Resource Mobilization:* Successful entrepreneurship requires the ability to assemble and deploy resources effectively, including financial capital, human capital, and social networks.

- *Risk-Taking:* Entrepreneurship involves taking calculated risks, stepping into uncertainty, and embracing failure as a natural part of the learning process. I say it's waking up every day and betting on yourself and the vision that only you can see.

- *Action Orientation*: Entrepreneurs are action-oriented individuals who translate ideas into action, taking decisive steps to bring their vision to fruition.

- *Innovation:* Central to entrepreneurship is innovation, the ability to develop new ideas, products, services, or business models that create value and differentiate from existing offerings.

Defining Entrepreneurship in Public Health

When we think of entrepreneurship, we often associate it with business and the creation of new products or services. However, in the context of public health, entrepreneurship takes on a unique meaning and purpose. It is about identifying innovative solutions to address the most pressing health challenges facing our communities. It's working closely with organizations and stakeholders to understand the needs of the community and then developing tailored solutions that will have a real and lasting impact on people's lives. But it's not just about coming up with ideas. Entrepreneurship in public health is also about taking action and making those ideas a reality. It's about being proactive, resilient, and adaptable in the face of challenges. It's about creating sustainable programs and initiatives that will continue to benefit communities long after their initial implementation and long after the funding ends.

What is Public Health Entrepreneurship?

In short, "public health entrepreneurship is the application of entrepreneurial skills to advance the public health mission" (Becker et al., 2019). It is a dynamic and innovative approach that combines the principles of public health with entrepreneurial principles, practices, and strategies for public health initiatives and projects to address health disparities, promote well-being, and create sustainable solutions to public health challenges. It is often used interchangeably with "social entrepreneurship", which is driven by social innovation and the desire to produce social change. Public health

Entrepreneurship in the Context of Public Health

entrepreneurship is a form of social entrepreneurship (Chahine, 2021).

A public health entrepreneur is an individual who leverages their expertise in public health to identify, develop, and implement entrepreneurial solutions aimed at improving health outcomes and fostering positive societal changes, particularly those related to underserved or vulnerable populations. *Most public health entrepreneurs work as public health consultants.*

What Does a Public Health Consultant Do?

Generally speaking, a consultant is someone who gives specialized advice and guidance in their area of expertise. Anyone can be a consultant in just about any area they want to: business development, marketing, IT, communications, legal, education, and so on. A public health consultant works with groups and organizations to help them determine what ways they can improve the public's health or a population's health. Public health consultants often establish business models or ventures to sustain their initiatives as they work with organizations. These models can include nonprofit organizations, for-profit ventures, social enterprises, or consultancy services. This is what makes a public health consultant a public health entrepreneur.

A public health consultant can take on various roles and responsibilities to drive positive change in the public health landscape and they play a crucial role in the field of public health by providing specialized expertise, guidance, and support to organizations, governments, healthcare institutions, and communities. Their primary focus is to help clients address public health challenges, improve health outcomes, and implement effective strategies and programs.

Public health consultants often bring a multidisciplinary approach to their work, drawing from expertise in areas such as epidemiology, biostatistics, health education, policy analysis, and program management. Their role is dynamic and adaptable, as they tailor their services to meet the specific needs and goals of their clients, ultimately contributing to the

Entrepreneurship in the Context of Public Health

improvement of public health at local, regional, and national levels.

The work of a public health consultant can include anything from conducting needs assessments to program development, to training and workforce development, to policy work, and so on. Below are examples of the kind of work that public health consultants do. This list is not exhaustive:

- *Assessment and Analysis:* Public health consultants conduct thorough assessments and data analysis to identify public health issues, health disparities, and areas of concern. They evaluate existing health programs, policies, and systems to determine their effectiveness.

- *Strategic Planning:* Public health consultants develop strategic plans and recommendations based on their assessments. They work with clients to set clear objectives, define goals, and create actionable plans for addressing public health concerns.

- *Program Development:* Public health consultants assist in designing, developing, and implementing public health programs and interventions. This includes creating evidence-based strategies, selecting appropriate interventions, and tailoring programs to specific populations or communities.

- *Policy Analysis:* Public health consultants analyze public health policies, regulations, and legislation to assess their impact on health outcomes. They provide recommendations for policy changes or improvements to promote better public health.

- *Research and Evaluation:* Public health consultants may conduct research studies and program evaluations to measure the effectiveness of health interventions. They use data to inform decision-making and make adjustments as needed.

Entrepreneurship in the Context of Public Health

- *Community Engagement:* Public health consultants engage with communities and stakeholders to ensure that public health initiatives are culturally sensitive, inclusive, and responsive to community needs. They facilitate partnerships and collaboration to enhance program outcomes.

- *Training and Capacity Building:* Public health consultants provide training and capacity-building services to public health professionals and organizations. This includes workshops, seminars, and educational sessions to enhance skills and knowledge in the field.

- *Health Communication:* Public health consultants develop communication strategies and campaigns to raise awareness, educate the public, and promote healthy behaviors. They may also create materials and content for health promotion.

- *Data Management and Surveillance:* Public health consultants assist in establishing data collection and surveillance systems to monitor health trends, track disease outbreaks, and assess the impact of interventions.

- *Quality Improvement:* Public health consultants work on quality improvement initiatives within healthcare settings, public health agencies, or organizations to enhance the delivery of healthcare services and programs.

- *Emergency Preparedness:* Public health consultants help clients prepare for and respond to public health emergencies, such as natural disasters or disease outbreaks. They develop emergency response plans and protocols.

Entrepreneurship in the Context of Public Health

- *Grant Writing and Funding:* Public health consultants assist organizations in identifying funding opportunities, preparing grant proposals, and securing financial resources for public health projects.

In essence, a public health entrepreneur is a change agent who combines public health expertise with entrepreneurial thinking to create meaningful, sustainable, and scalable solutions that contribute to better health outcomes and social well-being. Their work is characterized by a deep commitment to addressing health disparities and promoting health equity through innovative and purpose-driven approaches.

As a public health professional, embracing entrepreneurship can bring numerous benefits. Rather than relying solely on traditional methods and limited resources, you can tap into innovative ideas to transform public health in communities. Public health entrepreneurship allows you to think outside of the box and find creative solutions to complex health issues, solutions that are not confined by the traditional constraints of public health.

In the context of public health, entrepreneurship isn't merely about starting a business; it's a paradigm shift that propels one's passion and expertise to new heights. By being open-minded and willing to take risks, you can constantly evolve and adapt your approaches to effectively address the changing needs of the communities you serve. While entrepreneurship may not be the first thing that comes to mind when thinking about public health, it is a crucial aspect of driving progress and creating lasting impact.

The Entrepreneurial Process
The entrepreneurial process is a systematic journey that entrepreneurs undertake to transform ideas into successful ventures. This process typically involves several stages, each with its own set of tasks, challenges, and opportunities. The stages of the entrepreneurial process are significant in shaping a successful venture. The steps include idea

generation, opportunity evaluation, planning, implementation, and growth.

Idea Generation involves brainstorming, exploring, and generating innovative ideas that have the potential to address unmet needs or solve pressing problems. This first step is important because idea generation lays the foundation for entrepreneurship by sparking creativity and identifying opportunities for value creation.

Example: Public health professionals may generate ideas for new interventions, programs, or technologies to address health disparities, promote preventive care, or improve access to healthcare services.

Opportunity Evaluation or Idea Validation happens when entrepreneurs evaluate the feasibility, market potential, and viability of their ideas by conducting market research, analyzing competition, and assessing risks and opportunities. This stage is important because opportunity assessment helps entrepreneurs validate their ideas, refine their value proposition, and identify potential obstacles or challenges to address.

Example: Public health entrepreneurs may assess community needs, epidemiological data, and stakeholder insights to identify opportunities for intervention and prioritize initiatives with the greatest potential for impact.

Planning involves developing a comprehensive business plan, a business model canvas, or a strategic roadmap that outlines the goals, objectives, resources, and timelines for launching and scaling a business venture. Planning is instrumental because it serves as a plan of action, guiding decision-making, resource allocation, and risk management throughout the entrepreneurial journey.

Example: Public health initiatives require detailed planning to define program objectives, target populations, intervention strategies, and evaluation metrics, ensuring alignment with public health goals and priorities.

Implementation is the stage where entrepreneurs execute their plans, mobilize resources, and bring their ideas to life through action and execution. Implementation transforms ideas into tangible outcomes, enabling entrepreneurs to test, iterate, and refine their strategies based on real-world feedback and experience.

Example: Public health entrepreneurs implement interventions, programs, or campaigns to promote health education, disease prevention, healthcare access, or community empowerment, collaborating with stakeholders and leveraging existing infrastructure and resources.

Growth involves scaling and expanding the venture, increasing its reach, impact, and sustainability over time through innovation, partnerships, and strategic investments. Growth is essential for long-term success, enabling entrepreneurs to maximize their impact, capture new opportunities, and achieve sustainable outcomes.

Example: Successful public health initiatives undergo growth through replication, adaptation, and dissemination of best practices, expanding their reach to new populations, geographic areas, or sectors, and catalyzing broader systemic change.

Applying the Entrepreneurial Process to Public Health Consulting

Public health consultants navigate a similar entrepreneurial journey as they identify unmet needs, innovate solutions, and deliver impactful consulting services. By spotting pain points, employing creative problem-solving, and tailoring solutions to client needs, public health consultants drive positive change to advance health equity.

Spotting Unmet Needs: Pain points are essentially unmet needs or challenges in public health. Identifying these pain points provides the foundation for spotting opportunities for innovation. Public health consultants can ask themselves, *"How can I address these unmet needs and alleviate these pain points?"*

Using Creative Problem-Solving: Innovations in public health consulting involve creative problem-solving. Public health consultants take the pain points they've identified and explore novel approaches, technologies, or interventions to address them effectively. They turn these challenges into opportunities for positive change.

Developing Tailored Consulting Solutions: Public health consultants often offer consulting services to organizations or communities seeking solutions to their challenges. By understanding the pain points and challenges faced by their clients, entrepreneurs can tailor consulting solutions that directly address these issues. These solutions are designed to bring about meaningful change and improvement.

The Link Between Entrepreneurship and Innovation
It is estimated that it takes 17 years to scale up 14% of public health innovations, due largely to the limitations presented by the traditional grant-based system for public health research and development. This suggests that we need a more agile, dynamic system to foster and scale public health innovation in public health solutions (Huang et al., 2022). Entrepreneurship and innovation are interconnected, with entrepreneurship serving as a vehicle for translating innovative ideas into tangible outcomes. The ability to identify pain points and turn them into opportunities for innovation is a central aspect of effective public health consulting and entrepreneurship. It's about understanding the challenges, empathizing with those affected, and leveraging innovative thinking to create solutions that make a meaningful impact on public health.

A novel approach suggested by Huang and team considers innovating from the perspective of true community needs and values. Lessons on innovation based on human- and community-centered design suggest there is an opportunity to leverage bottom-up and asset-based approaches. One strategy aligned with this thinking is to harness and cultivate untapped innovations in communities which means solutions will be created by individuals with lived experience of the problems they seek to solve. Public health entrepreneurs possess this understanding of the true needs and pain points of a community. Public health entrepreneurs drive innovation by:

- Identifying unmet needs (or pain points) in public health systems and communities.

- Developing novel interventions, technologies, or business models to address these challenges.

- Testing and refining innovative solutions through experimentation, iteration, and feedback.

- Scaling successful innovations to reach broader populations and maximize impact.

- Catalyzing systemic change by challenging entrenched norms, policies, and practices that perpetuate health inequities.

The Current Public Health Consulting Landscape
The rise of the self-employed consultant and entrepreneur marks a significant shift in how expertise is shared, solutions are developed, and impact is measured. While not much has been written on the topic of the public health consulting landscape, Roman et. al conducted their research on "Describing the Self-Employed Public Health Consultant and Entrepreneur Workforce in the United States – A Survey Snapshot for Consultants" (2023). The findings of this pivotal survey snapshot shed light on the unconventional profession of public health consulting and its unique paths. By understanding the current state of the public health consulting landscape, we uncover the opportunities and challenges that lie ahead for this career path. This knowledge empowers us, as a community of public health professionals, to support one

another, advocate for the value of our work, and continue to innovate in our approaches to public health challenges.

Among the participants who took part in the survey performed by Roman and team, 119 individuals identified themselves as public health consultants. A significant majority of these consultants were women, making up 92% of the respondents. Regarding racial diversity, 74% of the participants were White, while Black, Asian, and Hispanic consultants represented 16%, 7%, and 6% of the group, respectively. The educational background of these consultants is notably high, with 67% holding master's degrees and 28% possessing doctorate degrees. The survey also revealed an even split in their professional engagement, with half of the respondents working as full-time consultants and the other half dedicating themselves to part-time consulting. Additional information gleaned from this research is below:

What is motivating public health professionals to leave the traditional public health workforce?
- Opportunity to choose topics or projects of interests
- Option for more flexible work hours
- Autonomy to create own work environment and processes
- Option to work remotely

How much money do public health consultants make?
- Average Hourly Rate - $120 USD
- Average Annual Revenue
    - Full-time: $109,106
    - Part-time: $40,941
- Average Net Income
    - Full-time: $80,268

- Part-time: $28,323

Pricing Strategies Used
- 83% use hourly rates
- 68% use project based rates
- 18% use fee for products
- 10% use retainers

Note: *Many consultants use these strategies in combination.*

Who hires public health consultants?
- Nonprofit Organizations - 69%
- Academic Institutions - 39%
- Other Consultants - 38%
- Government Agencies - 36%

What services do public health consultants offer?
- Most common services:
  - Training and capacity building
  - Meeting planning and/or facilitation
  - Program design, planning, and implementation
  - Program evaluation
  - Writing
  - Data analysis

- Least common services:
  - Policy and advocacy
  - Workforce development

- Instructional design
- Career development

What challenges do public health consultants encounter when starting their business?
- How to set up a business (e.g., choosing the right legal structure)
- Navigating the transition period (e.g., having sufficient cash flow for start-up)
- Getting work (e.g., marketing services)
- Psychosocial challenges (e.g., navigating imposter syndrome)

What are the professional development needs for consultants and entrepreneurs?
- Most common needs
    - Budget and tax planning
    - Writing contracts and scopes of work
    - Personal branding
    - Business planning
    - Marketing
    - Client management

What might motivate public health consultants to return to a traditional workforce?
- Desire for consistent income
- Desire for benefits like insurance, paid leave, retirement
- Flexibility in work location and scheduling
- Desire to work in a team environment

How can this data collected from this survey empower public health consultants and entrepreneurs?

For starters, it offers us a map of benchmarks to better understand where we stand in comparison to other consultants in other industries. Second, there's the insight into the market landscape. Identifying where the market may be crowded and identifying areas where there is room to grow allows consultants to strategically position their services. This data also unites us, enabling us to advocate for the resources and recognition we deserve, such as a centralized membership association dedicated to our unique needs. It also allows us to understand the income potential for those just starting, so we have insights to not only launch successfully but also to sustain and grow our businesses year after year.

How can this information transform the world of public health, academia, and workforce development?

Imagine public health organizations discovering the vast possibilities that independent consulting offers. This insight can open doors to innovative solutions and services that were previously unexplored. Employers, on the other hand, can harness this knowledge to attract and keep the best minds, ensuring their teams are strong and effective in traditional public health roles. Training centers have a golden opportunity to tailor their programs more precisely. By understanding the specific needs of consultants and entrepreneurs, they can design courses that truly make a difference, equipping professionals with the skills they need to thrive. Academia can weave this real-life data into their courses and educators can offer students a glimpse into the entrepreneurial side of public health. This not only enriches their learning experience but also sparks curiosity, leading to new research questions that delve into this unique sector of the public health workforce.

The information gleaned from this survey isn't just data. It's a beacon that guides the future of public health, shaping a workforce that's innovative, skilled, and ready to meet the challenges of tomorrow.

I want to extend my heartfelt gratitude to my public health colleagues for generously dedicating their time, expertise, and effort to conducting, compiling, and analyzing this research. Your willingness to share these insights so openly to advance and innovate the field of public health is deeply appreciated.

Should You Consider Public Health Consulting?
You can become a public health consultant by having the right education, experience, and exposure. I decided to become a public health consultant after 10 years of nursing and five years of implementing numerous successful public health programs in local and state health departments. You should consider public health consulting if....

- You have at least three (3) years of experience in healthcare, public health, or the health and wellness industry.

- You have worked for government, healthcare, non-profits, educational institutions, or a combination of all the above.

- You want to leverage your skills and expertise into a business that allows you to live and serve others on your own terms.

- You want to put your years of education, and all those degrees and certifications, to better use.

- You want to make a difference doing things you're passionate about while getting paid handsomely for it.

- You are ready to offer your expertise to businesses and organizations as a public health consultant or freelancer.

Entrepreneurship in the Context of Public Health

- You've been thinking about starting a public health consulting business for years and now you're ready to take action!

In the next chapter, I will share some pivotal moments in my career that ultimately led to my decision to embark on my entrepreneurial journey.

Chapter 3:
My Journey into Public Health Entrepreneurship

The Disillusioned Dreamer
I dedicated more than a decade to nursing before surrendering to a new calling in public health. I encountered professional challenges in both my nursing and public health careers that ultimately led me to pursue self-employment. No single event propelled my trajectory into entrepreneurship. Instead, it was more like a series of unfortunate events that occurred over many years.

Since I was already working as a Nurse Tech at the Veterans Administration (VA) Hospital, I decided to apply for a full-time position there after graduating. My nursing career exposed me to a variety of nursing specialties. I worked a one-year stint in the surgical intensive care unit as a new graduate nurse, then spent a few years providing care on a long-term unit the VA Hospital calls the Community Living Center (CLC). I spent my last few nursing years working as the clinic coordinator for an outpatient endocrinology clinic. As most nurses do, I worked a lot of overtime and would occasionally "moonlight" on other floors that were short-handed and needed nursing staff. Some of the hospital wards I liked a lot, like pre-operative care, post-operative care, and the hospice/palliative care floor. But some of the wards I didn't particularly care for, like medical/surgical, cardiology, and oncology units, to name a few.

When I think back to the first ten years of my nursing career, entrepreneurship never crossed my mind, not even once. Why would it? After all, nursing was my passion and I had worked hard to establish myself as a competent and compassionate healthcare professional. I was proud of my career in nursing. I was proud to be called a nurse. I was proud to serve those who served others, our nation's veterans. But deep down inside, something was missing.

I began becoming disillusioned with nursing during my time in the CLC. A Community Living Center is a VA Nursing Home. It's a place where Veterans can receive skilled nursing care in a home-like environment for patients requiring a longer hospital stay. Veterans may stay in CLCs for a short time or, in rare instances, for the rest of their lives. The patients that I cared for received wound care, respite care, hospice/palliative care, and rehabilitative services. It was during my time in the CLC that I came to understand that health primarily happens outside of the hospital's walls. I had not yet heard the term "social determinants of health" and therefore, had no language to articulate what I was starting to understand. I knew the care that we were providing on the unit was simply conventional, addressing specific diseases or acute symptoms with short-term treatments, medications, and procedures. I felt like the care I was providing was nothing more than a band-aid that would be ripped off as soon as the patient was discharged home, and I began to feel hopeless. The dreams I once had of being that super nurse who would fix all the patients who walked through the hospital's doors had slowly diminished. I thought a change in environment was what I needed -that I could take my skills to another floor, and they would be put to better use.

As soon as I graduated with my bachelor's degree in nursing, I started applying to other jobs. I wanted to go to a nursing position where I could realize my dream of making a difference in my patients' lives. I obtained a new position in the hospital's outpatient endocrinology clinic where most of my patients had diabetes and accompanying comorbidities, like obesity and hypertension. In my new role, I not only facilitated the day-to-day operations of the clinic and performed clinical procedures, I also got the opportunity to provide diabetes education to patients and their family members.

Over the years, I came to know all of my patients on a first-name basis. At the clinic, patients with diabetes were scheduled for return visits every six months if their blood glucose levels were on target and every three months for those still working towards their goals. Seeing patients only two to four times per year made me wonder how our patients were managing their diabetes and other chronic conditions the rest of the time. It was during these moments of reflection that I began to see the delicate connection between healthcare and social/societal factors. I came to understand that missed appointments often weren't a matter of forgetfulness, but rather the result of lacking transportation to the clinic. I discovered that it wasn't always a lack of will that prevented patients from taking their insulin correctly, but sometimes a lack of understanding of how to adjust their insulin based on their carbohydrate intake. And I realized that when a patient didn't follow a low-fat, low-carb diet, it wasn't necessarily defiance against medical advice, or them being "noncompliant" but a matter of eating what was financially accessible to them.

These insights were pivotal for me, highlighting the complex interplay between medical advice and the SDoH. This is when I started to connect the dots. This is when I realized the care that I was providing to patients needed to extend beyond the hospital's walls. This is when I came to understand that social circumstances, behavioral choices, economic challenges, cultural misunderstandings, geographic barriers, and even the unconscious differences in the way providers treat patients from varying segments of society all have a major impact on health outcomes. It wasn't long after getting the position in the endocrinology clinic that I started an MPH program and obtained my certification in diabetes education. Two years later, I would end up at the third-largest health department in the United States.

Falling Out of Love with Serving
I considered myself lucky when I landed my first role in public health. In fact, I'd like to think I was blessed. I had asked God to send me a job that combined my love for nursing, public health, and diabetes (by that time I was a Certified Diabetes Educator). With 10 years of nursing under my belt, experience

in the inpatient, outpatient, and community settings as a volunteer nurse, a couple of certifications, a shiny new MPH degree, and divine intervention, I secured a job as a Chief Nurse at the Houston Health Department (HHD) in the Office of Chronic Disease Prevention and Management, overseeing the Colorectal Cancer Awareness and Screening (COCAS) program and the Diabetes Awareness and Wellness Network (DAWN) program. I absolutely LOVED working as a Program Manager, until it no longer loved me back.

My role as Chief Nurse and Program Manager was my first introduction to health promotion programming and implementation and I THRIVED IN IT! Not to toot my own horn, but TOOT TOOT! During my time at the health department, I worked on various community health initiatives and collaborated with other departments and community organizations to implement evidence-based interventions aimed at improving health outcomes in underserved populations. I witnessed firsthand how social determinants such as poverty, education, and access to healthcare can significantly impact an individual or community. I also witnessed how communities can be empowered and uplifted if provided with the right assistance and supported with tools that help to foster self-efficacy. I never felt closer to the community than I did in my role as Chief Nurse at HHD, and I am forever grateful for the experiences and lessons learned during my time there. Looking back on things now, I can say the honeymoon phase ended right about the six-month mark. But like any relationship when you are in love, you do what you can to make it work and stick it out with hopes that things will get better.

This might sound like an exaggeration but working 50-hour weeks is pretty standard in public health leadership roles. And if I managed to limit my workweek to just 50 hours, I considered that a win. The reality is, when your days are filled with back-to-back meetings, the real work doesn't start until after you've made dinner, settled your family for the night, and finally have a moment to yourself. And for those of us in roles that involve community engagement, weekends often mean

My Journey into Public Health Entrepreneurship

being out in the community at health fairs, community forums, and other community events. This was my routine for four years. My evenings were spent with my laptop open, responding to emails, drafting reports, and frantically writing grants to secure funding for my team and our projects, among countless other tasks that fall on the shoulders of a Program Manager. Despite the demanding hours and weekend work, it would have all been worth it if it meant having well-funded programs, adequate staffing, the support and appreciation of leadership, and managers who valued work-life balance. Sadly, that's not the reality for many in public health. More often than not, our work is underfunded, understaffed, and lacks the support of leadership that expects us to "do whatever it takes to get the job done as long as we don't clock more than 40 hours a week." Knowing full well we can't get everything that needs to be done in 40 hours.

During my time at HHD, I co-created and spearheaded the development, implementation, and evaluation of several health promotion programs including diabetes prevention and management, hypertension, stress management, tobacco cessation, and nutrition education programs. Additionally, I oversaw the development of several partnerships and a network of healthcare and community partners that served African American and Hispanic populations in the Third Ward of Houston. This increase in formal partnerships led to a 362% increase in referrals into the Diabetes Programs!

As I began to get more comfortable in my roles, my ideas for my programs began to get more creative and innovative. While this is a positive for most organizations, this is not always the case in public health. In fact, it can often be difficult to implement new and innovative ideas within the confines of traditional public health practices and funding sources. If I'm honest, I found government bureaucracy frustrating (and that's putting it lightly). I despised having to go through the many levels of approval to get the simplest things done. I dreaded the tedious reporting requirements for relatively small amounts of grant funding, and the overall inability to make timely decisions that ultimately impacted the communities that we were serving. I started "asking for forgiveness, not permission" to ensure that my staff and my community could be served timely and appropriately.

In 2017, I hit a brick wall. At the time, it felt like a nervous breakdown, but looking back, I understand now that it was burnout. After a five-week leave of absence, a prescription for anti-anxiety medication, and several therapy sessions later, I knew something had to give. I was at a crossroads. I knew staying in my position was harming my mental, physical, and emotional health. I didn't want to abandon my team or the community we served, but I also knew that if I could manage multiple staff, initiatives, and budgets for my department, maybe, just maybe, I could do the same for myself. People often ask how I manage all the projects I do now as an entrepreneur. My answer is simple: my experience in public health, specifically public health leadership, laid the groundwork for this.

A Perceived Conflict of Interest
I left HHD after four years to work for the Texas Department of State Health Services as a Diabetes Nurse Consultant. My family relocated to Austin, Texas and I took a $13,000 pay cut for peace of mind and a new beginning. In my new role, I participated in planning at the state level providing clinical expertise in the prevention and management of diabetes and related chronic diseases. While I gained a wealth of experience in stakeholder engagement and providing technical assistance (i.e. consulting) to public health systems and healthcare organizations using a multidisciplinary and multi-sectoral approach, this position was the least challenging position I'd encountered in my career. The pace was slow, the days long, and I found myself craving more stimulation. Frankly, I was bored. The most exciting part of the job was working with organizations throughout the state to help them integrate a virtual component of their diabetes education programs. Keep in mind, this was pre-COVID, so it was challenging for many

organizations, and fascinating for me. The obstacles faced by health departments and healthcare systems were significant, from cost and privacy concerns to bureaucratic hurdles. Yet, I got to spend my days (and often my nights) researching virtual platforms, HIPAA-compliant software programs, and effective online curricula and training methods. Every day, I would share the information and resources that I learned with our clients who didn't seem any closer to implementing than they did the week before.

One day I went home frustrated and told my husband, "It can't be this hard to provide virtual diabetes education. You know what? I'm going to do it myself. I'm bored anyway, I'm going to start another business." I had attempted business twice before this point, but both ventures were unsuccessful. Over the next five months, I threw myself into providing virtual chronic disease education classes, free webinars, and a virtual Diabetes Prevention Program (DPP) to whoever was willing to join—initially, this was mostly my family. By the fifth month, I had managed to enroll five clients in my low-cost virtual DPP. Then, COVID-19 changed everything. Diabetes prevention education was no longer a priority for my participants, and I recognized the urgent need to pivot my business if I wanted to start seeing profits.

Having recently earned my certification to train Community Health Workers (CHWs), I saw an opportunity and pursued it. I reached out to five public health colleagues, inviting them to share their expertise at a virtual summit. Within two weeks, we organized the first Virtual CHW Summit, the theme was "Preparing CHWs to Respond to COVID-19." I thought we would be lucky if 100 people signed up for the event and even remember telling my colleagues as much. To my surprise, almost 800 attendees signed up for the free 5-day event. It was then that I knew I had a service that was in high demand and when my business transitioned from providing health education to workforce development.

A couple of months later, my manager asked to see me in her office. At the time, I didn't suspect anything unusual but was quickly taken aback when she asked me about my business. I confirmed I had one, and she instructed me to fill out the outside employment form, which I did. Days later, she delivered the unsettling news that my entrepreneurial activities were seen as a *perceived conflict of interest* and my outside employment request had been denied. I was given an ultimatum: either shut down my business or face termination. I cried for three days. I felt so defeated. Just when my business was gaining traction and beginning to generate income, I was forced to shut it down to keep my job.

On the third day, my husband looked at me and asked, "Aren't you a nurse? Can't you work anywhere? You don't even like that job anyway." I looked at him shocked like he was speaking another language. He was right! I was a nurse (I am a nurse). By that time, I had been away from the bedside for five years and I had completely forgotten that nursing was a very viable option for me. I went straight to my home office and began typing up my letter of resignation. I spent a year at the State before deciding to leave. When I left, I secured a short-term position as an RN Care Manager at a Federally Qualified Health Center, which had no issues with my "side hustle". Later, I transitioned to a corporate role as a Training Specialist, where my outside business was also accepted. When I transitioned into full-time entrepreneurship, I was able to retain my former employer as a client for my public health consulting business.

Blazing My Own Trail
After 10 years of nursing and five years in public health leadership roles, I decided I owed it to myself to at least give full-time entrepreneurship a shot. After two and a half years, my side hustle salary had reached my full-time salary and I decided this was the best time to take the leap of faith.

My Journey into Public Health Entrepreneurship

I founded Umemba Health in 2019 and took full ownership as the full-time CEO in the Summer of '21. With my ability to devote my attention solely to my business, my mission was clear: to revolutionize public health with robust and comprehensive workforce development. Umemba Health is now a federally certified woman-owned small business with national certification as a women's business enterprise. Rooted in our core values of *purpose, people, and performance*, we help public health organizations and healthcare systems to educate their workforce, empower their leadership, and expand their community presence to elevate the lives of the individuals and communities they serve. In short, **we serve those who serve others.**

At Umemba Health, our mission is to advance health equity by helping public health professionals optimize their influence and impact, thereby contributing to individual development and organizational performance that leads to improved public health and population health outcomes. I will share more details about my public health consultancy, Umemba Health, and the services we provide in Chapter 4, so keep reading.

Reflecting on my journey, my path to public health entrepreneurship was not a straightforward one. It was a path marked with pivotal moments of profound insights and realizations. From my early days as a dedicated, yet disillusioned, nurse working within the confines of conventional healthcare to my roles in traditional public health settings where I became disenchanted by the constraints of public health service, each experience and every challenge had some part in sparking my entrepreneurial spirit. Each experience pushed me to think outside the box and find other ways to apply my skills and passions in new, impactful ways. The story of my entrepreneurial journey is a testament to the idea that with passion, perseverance, and a willingness to embrace change, it is possible to blaze a trail in public health on your own accord and do meaningful work to impact public health on your own terms.

If you don't build your dreams, someone else will hire you to build theirs. – Tony A. Gaskins, Jr.

Part 2 - Passion: Public Health Entrepreneurs – Profiles of Impact

Introduction
The goal of this book is simple: to expose public health professionals to the opportunities that exist in public health consulting and entrepreneurship, while simultaneously inspiring and empowering readers to embark on their own entrepreneurial journey. In Part 2 of this book, you will read the stories of remarkable individuals who, like me, have ventured into public health entrepreneurship and mastered the art of making impact and income. Through my story and the captivating narratives of three extraordinary women, you'll have the privilege of witnessing our unique experiences, profound insights, and invaluable lessons learned on our entrepreneurial paths. Each story is woven into a compelling narrative that showcases our passion, purpose, and perseverance while offering a glimpse into the diverse paths of public health consulting.

In Chapter 4, "**From Scrubs to Strategy**," I share more about my public health consulting business and the different ways that I serve to reduce health disparities and advance health equity.

In Chapter 5, "**Breaking Down Barriers to Support Healthy Communities**," you'll read Dr. Spinner's story of how her background and experiences have helped her find her niche in health equity consulting.

In Chapter 6, "**Bridging My Life's Purpose to Profit**," you'll read about Jometra Hawkins, a Lupus Warrior with humble beginnings whose lived experiences empowered her to become a powerful advocate and community health translator.

In Chapter 7, "**Taking Action Beyond Data Insights**," you will meet Vanessa DaCosta whose education and work experience have taken her around the world and back in pursuit of health equity.

Join Jovonni, Jometra, Vanessa, and me as we share our journeys from Employee to CEO. I hope that as you read, you will draw strength and motivation from the shared experiences, triumphs, and challenges that unite us as fellow entrepreneurs in the field of public health. These stories are meant to serve as beacons of inspiration and empowerment, to introduce you to the possibilities that exist in public health consulting, and to serve as a reminder that your aspirations to effect positive change in public health are not merely dreams but tangible realities within your grasp.

Chapter 4:
From Scrubs to Strategy

Quisha Umemba, MPH, BSN, RN, CDCES, CHWI brings over 20 years of diverse experience to her roles as a Registered Nurse, Public Health Practitioner, and Entrepreneur. A visionary in the field of public health entrepreneurship, Quisha believes that public health professionals are uniquely positioned to serve the field of Public Health through entrepreneurship, leading the way for public health innovation. Her goal is to shed light on the pivotal role public health and healthcare professionals have in fostering innovation within the entrepreneurial landscape.

As the CEO of Umemba Health, Quisha helps public health organizations and healthcare systems to educate their workforce, empower their leadership, and expand their community presence. As the Principal for Quisha Umemba Consulting, Quisha teaches *helping professionals* to leverage their expertise, package their genius, and monetize their skillset so they can start, grow, and scale a profitable public health consulting business that makes impact and income. She is also the Founder of Umemba Health Foundation and Co-Founder of Diversity of Diabetes.

Quisha is a curriculum designer, expert facilitator, and highly qualified and experienced corporate trainer specializing in training of trainers, leadership development, and a range of personal and professional development topics. She is a sought-after presenter with a dynamic speaking style and an expert at engaging audiences virtually and in person. She is a subject matter expert in public health and population health strategies that support individual development and organizational performance, and she is a devoted servant leader and health equity advocate. Her life's mission is to empower, educate, and transform the lives of others. Her expertise in integrating Community Health Workers to address SDoH positions her as a leading voice in innovative healthcare strategies that advance health equity.

Quisha graduated from the University of Arkansas for Medication Sciences with a Master's in Public Health and obtained nursing degrees from the University of Phoenix and the University of Arkansas at Little Rock. Quisha lives in Dallas, Texas with her husband, son, and fur baby. She has authored the following books:

- *WIN Women in Nursing: The Entrepreneur's Anthology, Volume 1*
- *An Introduction to Entrepreneurship for Public Health Professionals*
- *Public Health Entrepreneurship: Navigating the Intersection of Purpose and Profit*

Business Websites:
www.umembahealth.com
www.quishaumemba.com

Business Facebook:
@umembahealth
@publichealthpreneur

Business Instagram:
@umembahealth
@quishaumemba

LinkedIn:
@umembahealth
@quishaumembaconsulting

From Scrubs to Strategy
Quisha Umemba

From Nursing to Public Health
I didn't have the traditional college experience. By the time I went to college, I was married with a toddler, so my college experience included nights and weekends while working full-time. After my Medical Assisting program, I enrolled in the local community college to complete prerequisite courses that I needed to apply for nursing school. Two years later, I enrolled in the University of Arkansas at Little Rock and completed a fast-track nursing program for my Associate Degree in Nursing. I worked as a floor nurse for a few years then enrolled into a 2-year nursing program at the University of Phoenix online. Once I decided I wanted to pursue a career in public health, I chose the University of Arkansas for Medical Sciences' MPH program with a focus on health education and human behavior. The MPH degree married perfectly with my nursing background and my experience in diabetes education so the transition into public health was a natural progression for me. My nursing background provided me with clinical knowledge and skills, while my MPH degree equipped me with a broader understanding of population health and community-based interventions.

My motivation to pursue a career in public health stems from my passion for helping people and making a positive impact on their lives. As a nurse, I saw firsthand the effects of chronic diseases such as diabetes, heart disease, and obesity on individuals and their families. I wanted to make a difference in preventing these diseases from occurring by focusing on population-level interventions through public health. I also saw the disparities in healthcare access and outcomes for marginalized communities, which fueled my desire to address health equity issues through public health initiatives.

My transition into public health consulting was the result of the frustration and burnout I experienced from the public health work culture. Despite my passion for promoting health equity and working towards social justice, I found myself constantly battling against bureaucratic red tape, funding constraints, and conflicting interests. I knew that something needed to change for me to continue making a meaningful impact in the field of public health, so I decided to pursue a career in consulting. My transition into public health consulting started as a "side hustle". I built my business while still working full-time, which I recommend as the best way to transition into public health entrepreneurship. Having a side hustle allows you to keep your main source of income while building your public health consulting business.

How and Who I Serve
My niche in public health consulting is workforce development, often termed "training and capacity building" within the field of public health. Whether you resonate with one term or the other, they encapsulate the same concept: employee training, professional development opportunities, and continuing education programs. In public health, continuous learning and skill enhancement are not just options; they are necessities. The goal of my training and consulting solutions is to improve individual development and organizational performance and to help individuals and organizations get an ROI: Return on Impact!

At Umemba Health, our most requested services include curriculum development, course creation, and workshop facilitation. We utilize a blend of conventional, experiential, and transformational training approaches to craft engaging educational content delivered across diverse platforms to provide exceptional learning experiences that nurture talent and create lasting impact inside the organization and within the community. We are renowned for our innovative community health worker training and certification programs, but we also offer a variety of consulting services including:
- Curriculum Adaptation or Redesign
- Health Equity and Health Promotion Programs
- CHW Program Consulting

- Clinical Integration Consulting
- Continuing Education (CE) Accreditation Consulting
- Leadership Development
- Executive Coaching
- And more

Our clients include small and large non-profit organizations, foundations, public health entities, academic institutions, and corporate organizations. Most services provided to our clients include a combination of training and consulting services. Notable clients that we have served include Project Hope, the Epilepsy Foundation, the Medical University of South Carolina, the University of Arkansas for Medical Sciences, the University of Minnesota, the California Black Health Network, the Young Women's Christian Association (YWCA), Heluna Health, Signify Health (acquired by CVS Health), and the National Association of County and City Health Officials, to name a few.

A Day in the Life
My role as CEO includes overseeing the day-to-day operations of projects, including budgeting, resource allocation, and team coordination to ensure project success and client satisfaction. Four years into business now means that approximately 40% of my time is spent in lead-generation activities, approximately 40% is spent in revenue-generating activities, and the remaining 20% is spent doing administrative work.

For me, lead generation consists of:
- Conducting discovery sessions and engaging with clients to understand their needs, goals, and challenges related to their public health initiatives or projects.
- Hosting educational webinars or workshops to showcase my company's expertise, engage with

participants, and collect contact information from attendees who are interested in learning more about our products or services.

- Attending conferences, meetings, and networking events to connect with potential leads and establish relationships with prospects.

My revenue-generating activities include conducting sales pitches, responding to RFPs, writing business proposals, and meeting with current or former clients to discuss ways to retain them as clients. The most important revenue-generating activities include working on client deliverables:

- Conducting assessments or evaluations to identify gaps, challenges, and opportunities in public health programs or systems.

- Developing project plans, timelines, and strategies in collaboration with clients to address identified needs and achieve project objectives.

- Gathering and analyzing data, literature, and evidence to inform decision-making and recommendations for public health interventions.

- Designing, implementing, and managing public health programs, interventions, or initiatives aimed at improving health outcomes or addressing specific health issues.

- Providing training, technical assistance, and capacity-building support to clients and partner organizations to enhance their knowledge, skills, and resources in public health practice.

Common Challenges in Public Health Consulting
In my experience working with organizations in the public health or healthcare sector, I frequently encounter two significant challenges. First are the organizations that either

have never engaged consultants before or have had negative experiences with consultants in the past. I have encountered resistance to implementing recommendations and difficulty gaining support from key stakeholders when either of these is the case.

Secondly, some organizations work heavily with multiple consultants simultaneously. I personally have a big issue with this. Working with an organization that employs numerous consultants presents major hurdles for a public health consultant. For one, there is a lack of coordination among the various consultants and that often leads to conflicting recommendations and strategies making the consulting process challenging.

Other noteworthy challenges include projects that lack proper scoping. Without clear boundaries, consultants usually end up spending more time than planned on a project. Additionally, projects involving multiple departments and stakeholders with competing priorities and separate agendas can pose significant management challenges. Delays caused by waiting for feedback from various teams can disrupt project timelines and ultimately affect project deadlines.

Remaining Relevant
Staying up to date on the latest trends in public health is one of the greatest challenges for a public health consultant who is no longer employed in a public health organization. Within a public health agency, you're at the forefront of industry developments, innovations, and shifts in trends. However, when you transition to working independently as a public health entrepreneur, this dynamic changes. Here are some ways that I stay "in the loop":
- Participating in continuing education programs, workshops, seminars, and webinars offered by professional organizations, academic institutions, and industry associations. These programs provide opportunities to learn about emerging trends, research findings, and best practices in public health.

- Attending professional networking events helps to build and maintain professional relationships with peers, colleagues, mentors, and industry experts in the public health field. Networking events, conferences, and online communities offer valuable opportunities to exchange knowledge, share insights, and stay informed about industry developments.

- Subscribing to industry publications, journals, newsletters, and blogs that cover topics relevant to public health. Reading academic journals, trade magazines, and online publications can provide insights into current research, policy changes, and innovative practices shaping the field.

- Leveraging online resources and platforms like public health websites, forums, and public health social media accounts to access timely information. They also allow you to engage with thought leaders in public health.

- Following reputable organizations, influencers, and experts on platforms like LinkedIn to stay updated on news, trends, and discussions in the field.

- Attending conferences, symposiums, and professional events focused on public health topics. These gatherings offer opportunities to hear from leading experts, participate in panel discussions, and learn about the latest research findings and advancements in the field.

- Collaborating with academic institutions, research organizations, government agencies, and non-profit organizations to access resources, data, and expertise. Partnering with stakeholders in the public health ecosystem can facilitate knowledge exchange, collaboration on projects, and access to valuable insights and resources.

Strategies for Building Relationships
Relationships are built on trust, communication, and understanding. My first goal when working with clients and stakeholders is to establish trust. I do this by under-promising and over-delivering, consistently producing high-quality services, being transparent in my communication, and following through on promises and commitments.

Communicating effectively is the key component in building strong relationships with clients and stakeholders. I actively listen to clients and stakeholders, address any concerns or issues promptly, and keep them informed about any changes or updates in services or policies. Understanding the needs and perspectives of clients and stakeholders is also crucial in building and maintaining strong relationships. To do this, I take the time to get to know them, their values, and their goals. This allows me to better tailor services to meet the specific needs of the organization. I also seek feedback from clients and stakeholders, during and after the project wraps. This not only allows for continuous improvement but also shows that their opinions and experiences are valued.

Forecasting Public Health Trends
As my expertise lies in public health workforce development, the trends that I see in public health consulting are related to training and capacity building. I see a need to provide more emphasis in the following areas in the immediate future:

Leadership and soft skill development
According to the 2022 LinkedIn Global Talent Trends, 89% of recruiters say when a new hire doesn't work out, it usually comes down to a lack of soft skills. In fact, many

employers these days are prioritizing soft skills during the hiring process. Alexandra Levit, a workforce futurist, and author of *Humanity Works: Merging Technologies and People for the Workforce of the Future* said that "while most people are hired for their technical abilities, their soft skills give them "career durability," (Rockwood, 2021). These trends highlight the importance of leadership and soft skill development in the public health workforce. Additionally, public health efforts often require collaboration across interdisciplinary teams and organizations. Effective leadership and soft skills such as teamwork, conflict resolution, and negotiation are vital for fostering collaboration, leveraging diverse expertise, and achieving shared goals. Engaging with communities is a cornerstone of public health practice and another area where soft skills like empathy, cultural competence, trust building, and communication should be utilized.

Diversity, Equity, Inclusion, and Accessibility (DEIA)
DEIA has been at the forefront of public health discussions in recent years. With the increasing awareness and recognition of systemic inequities, there is a growing demand for organizations to prioritize diversity and inclusion efforts. This includes creating more inclusive spaces, providing equal opportunities for underrepresented groups, addressing bias and discrimination within healthcare systems, and of course, providing training and capacity building around these topics. As public health agencies and organizations strive towards more equitable and inclusive practices, there will be more requests for DEIA trainings and workshops. Examples include topics from implicit bias training to cultural competency workshops, all aimed at creating a more diverse and inclusive workforce and improving health outcomes for marginalized communities.

Technology and Artificial Intelligence
As the world becomes increasingly digital, technology is playing a crucial role in shaping public health. Tools like

artificial intelligence (AI) are being utilized to improve disease surveillance, streamline data collection and analysis, and enhance decision-making processes. In addition to AI, other digital tools such as mobile applications and telemedicine are also being utilized in public health. These advancements allow for more efficient and convenient access to healthcare services, especially for underserved populations. It also opens opportunities for remote monitoring and telehealth, increasing access to care for those who may not have easy access to physical healthcare facilities. While technology has the potential to greatly improve public health, it also brings challenges such as data privacy and security concerns as well as ethical considerations of using tools like AI. It will be important for public health professionals to be trained on how to use AI and other technology and also how to evaluate the impact of these tools on health equity.

Approaching Community-Centric Projects
Overall, our approach to developing and implementing effective public health strategies for diverse communities is rooted in education, empowerment, and community engagement. By educating the frontline workforce, empowering the organization's leaders, and expanding community presence, we help to create positive and sustainable change that improves health outcomes and enhances quality of life for all.

Educating the Frontline Workforce
We believe that empowering the frontline workforce with the knowledge and skills they need is essential for effective public health initiatives. Our approach involves providing targeted training and educational programs tailored to the specific needs and challenges of diverse communities. By equipping frontline workers with the necessary tools and information, they can better understand the unique needs of the communities they serve and deliver more culturally sensitive and effective interventions.

Empowering Organization's Leaders
Strong leadership is crucial for driving meaningful change and implementing sustainable public health strategies. Our approach focuses on empowering the organization's leaders with the skills, knowledge, and resources they need to champion public health initiatives within their communities. This may involve leadership development programs, coaching and mentoring, and strategic planning sessions. By empowering leaders to effectively communicate the importance of public health, mobilize resources, and engage stakeholders, they can create a culture of health and wellness within their organizations and inspire others to take action.

Expanding Community Presence
Building trust and credibility within diverse communities is essential for the success of public health initiatives. Our approach involves helping organizations expand their community presence through outreach, partnerships, and engagement activities. This may include providing technical assistance in organizing community events, conducting outreach campaigns, collaborating with local stakeholders, or recruiting community members to participate in surveys, research, community forums, etc. By actively engaging with the community, organizations can gain valuable insights, build relationships, and co-create solutions that address the specific needs and priorities of diverse communities.

Impacting the Community
Our favorite projects lie at the intersection of healthcare and public health because we recognize the inseparable link between these two domains. Also, because I like to find as many opportunities as I can to use my nursing skills. One of my favorite projects involved working with an urban community facing high rates of diabetes and limited access to healthcare services. Upon conducting a needs assessment and engaging with community members, it

became clear that there were multiple barriers preventing individuals from accessing diabetes management resources and preventive care.

My team and I conducted a comprehensive needs assessment to understand the specific challenges faced by the community. This involved gathering quantitative data on diabetes prevalence, healthcare utilization, and access to resources, as well as qualitative insights through interviews and focus groups with community members. We engaged with local healthcare providers, community organizations, faith-based groups, and other stakeholders to build partnerships and garner support for our initiatives. This collaborative approach ensured buy-in from key stakeholders and facilitated the sharing of resources and expertise. Then we developed culturally tailored educational materials and conducted outreach campaigns to raise awareness about diabetes prevention, management, and the importance of regular screenings. This included workshops, community events, and the dissemination of educational materials in multiple languages. Recognizing the limited access to healthcare services in the area, we worked with local providers to establish mobile clinics to bring diabetes screenings and preventive care directly to the community. This helped overcome transportation barriers and ensured that individuals could access care closer to home. Last, we implemented CHW-led support programs for individuals living with diabetes, including peer support groups, lifestyle coaching, and self-management workshops. These programs focused on empowering individuals to take control of their health and make sustainable lifestyle changes. Throughout the project, we collected data on key metrics such as diabetes screening rates, healthcare utilization, and self-management behaviors. This allowed us to track our progress, identify areas for improvement, and make adjustments to our strategies as needed.

As a result of these efforts, we saw tangible improvements in diabetes awareness, screening rates, and access to care within the community. More individuals were proactively managing their diabetes, leading to better health outcomes and a reduced burden on the healthcare system. This project highlighted the power of community-driven interventions and the importance of taking a holistic approach to address complex public health challenges. By leveraging local resources, engaging stakeholders, and empowering individuals, we were able to make a meaningful and lasting impact on the health of the community.

Another memorable project included engaging 2103 local health department grant recipients to help them expand the impact of their work by implementing strategies to integrate community health workers (CHW) through hiring, building resilient relationships, and centering health equity for sustainable public health programs in underserved communities. OT-2103 is a national initiative to address COVID-19 health disparities among populations at high-risk and underserved, including racial and ethnic minority populations and rural communities. For this project, we provided large-scale technical assistance and support by training and developing curricula and resources used by LHD staff. We provided several large group virtual training sessions, office hours, and 1:1 coaching, as well as the development of numerous CHW-related resources. Through this project, LHDs have been able to convene to share and discuss their CHW strategies, share best practices for working with CHWs related to data collection, service delivery, outreach, advocacy, or policy work, and develop, compile, or tailor existing resources, frameworks, or toolkits that CHWs can use to advance health equity in their community work.

Advice for New and Aspiring Public Health Consultants
Do not try to serve everyone.
Once you have decided on your target audience, stick with it. It can be tempting to want to work in other areas or with different audiences, but you want to stay in your zone of genius. You are not meant to serve everyone. Your product or service may not be suitable for everyone and trying to please everyone will only lead to diluted efforts and unsatisfied customers. Instead, focus on catering to the needs and wants of your target audience.

Do not try to work on every project.
It is important to understand that you cannot take on every project that comes your way. Trying to do so will only lead to burnout and compromised work quality. In the beginning, you may feel compelled to work on every project because you don't want to miss out on money, but all money is not good money! Instead, choose projects that align with your expertise and interests. Also, sometimes you will need to say no. Learn to say no to projects, clients, or partnerships that are not aligned with your values, that drain your energy, or do not fit into your overall business strategy. This will allow you to focus on what truly matters and avoid wasting time, energy, and resources on endeavors that may not bring you your desired results.

Don't think you have to know everything.
As much as we would like to be experts in every aspect of our business, it is simply not possible. Trying to do so will only lead to stress and frustration. Instead, focus on your strengths and seek help or collaborate with others where needed. This will not only allow you to produce better work but also create opportunities for growth and learning.

Don't think you have to be perfect.
Perfectionism can be a curse in the business world. While it is important to strive for quality, spending too much time trying to achieve perfection can hinder progress and lead to

missed opportunities. Instead, focus on continuous improvement and aim for progress rather than perfection. The key is to just keep going and work on getting better with time.

Do not try to go at it all alone.
The saying "teamwork makes the dream work" holds true in business as well as it does in sports. Trying to handle everything on your own can lead to burnout and compromise the success of your business. Instead, build a strong support system and delegate tasks when necessary. This will not only ease your workload but also foster collaboration and enhance the overall efficiency of your business.

Do show yourself grace.
Even when it comes with a step-by-step guide like this book, there are no hard and fast rules for entrepreneurship. Entrepreneurship is trial and error. The highs can be really high and the lows can be really low. Don't strive for perfection, but rather strive for progress and growth and give yourself grace to make mistakes and to learn from those mistakes.

Balancing Work and Life
Let me keep it real for a moment. Finding the right balance between work and life is something I've always found challenging. For me, work isn't just a job; it's a passion and, at times, a welcome distraction from the stressors of life. I genuinely love what I do, especially the creative aspects of my work. However, drawing the line on how much time I dedicate to work, especially from home, has been a tough journey. Balancing the demands of running my business with making time for family and friends has been my biggest hurdle.

As my business has grown over the past years, I've gotten better at saying "no" and in putting my well-being first. One strategy I've adopted to preserve my work-life balance is setting firm boundaries between my professional and personal life. Working remotely, I make it a point to log off my computer at the end of the day, close my office door, and put a physical sign on the outside of my home office to "Out of Office." I also mute my email notifications on my phone so they don't distract me.

Taking regular breaks throughout the day has been another game-changer for me. I wasn't always good at this, but now, whether it's stepping outside to walk my dog, meditating for a few minutes, or enjoying lunch away from my desk, these moments help me recharge and boost my productivity. In 2024, my husband and I agreed that taking breaks during the day was good, but we also needed to take more breaks away from the house (since we both work remotely). We've been intentional about scheduling a quarterly getaway so we can relax, unwind, and come back to work refreshed.

Perhaps the most significant change I've made to achieve a better work-life balance is adjusting my work schedule. I introduced "Minimal Mondays" at my company allowing us to work in the most relaxed manner possible, even in pajamas if we choose. More recently, we've started "Free Fridays," effectively moving to a four-day workweek. With this schedule, we only have two days available for client and partner meetings, giving us two solid days to focus on our work and meet client deliverables. These adjustments have not only helped me maintain a healthier balance but also allowed me to stay passionate and productive in my work and personal life.

Essential Skills for Public Health Consultants
Naturally, public health consultants want to have a solid grasp of public health principles and the Core Competencies for Public Health Professionals is fundamental. However, the expertise should not stop there because a public health consultant needs to wear many

hats. Below are some of the critical skills they will need to complement their foundational knowledge:

- *Project Management:* The ability to lead projects from inception to completion is non-negotiable. This means crafting realistic timelines, managing resources efficiently, working seamlessly with teams, and achieving goals within set timeframes and budgets.

- *Communication and Negotiation:* Mastering the art of communication — both in writing and speaking — is crucial. A consultant must articulate complex ideas clearly to a variety of audiences, craft compelling reports, lead engaging presentations, and run effective workshops or training sessions.

- *Public Speaking:* Whether it's presenting findings to a board, leading a community workshop, or speaking at a conference, excellent public speaking skills ensure your message is heard and understood.

- *Finance Skills:* Understanding budgeting, financial management, and economic principles is essential, especially when planning projects or advocating for funding.

- *Management and Leadership:* Leading teams, inspiring colleagues, and managing resources effectively are all part of the consultant's role. Leadership skills help in guiding projects to success and fostering a positive work environment.

- *Marketing and Sales Skills:* Knowing how to market your services and sell your expertise is crucial for business growth. This includes understanding your target audience, crafting compelling messages, and building strong client relationships.

- *Knowledge of Business Operations:* A broad understanding of business operations, including strategic planning, operational efficiency, and customer service, ensures a consultancy runs smoothly and successfully.

Recommendations for Aspiring Public Health Consultants

Experience - I cannot state this enough, there's nothing like hands-on experience to pave the way for a thriving public health consulting business. Reflecting on my journey, every skill I honed while working with local and state health departments has been invaluable in my role as CEO. It's those real-world challenges and successes that have equipped me to lead and make impactful decisions every day.

Mentorship/Coaching – Looking back, it's clear that having business coaches positioned me for success, helping me to understand the business aspect of consulting and how to avoid common pitfalls. Additionally, a mentor with a background in public health consulting, particularly in your specialty, can offer profound insights and priceless advice.

Leadership Training – Steering public health initiatives and leading teams requires more than just a strong will; it demands refined leadership skills. I encourage seeking out programs or certifications specifically tailored to leadership in the healthcare or public health arenas. These opportunities not only bolster your ability to lead but also deepen your understanding of how to enact meaningful change within communities and organizations.

Certification(s) – For those already holding a degree in Public Health, I suggest considering at least one certification to complement your expertise (and to make you more competitive in the market). Whether it's Project Management, Certified in Public Health (CPH), Certified

Health Education Specialist (CHES), or Community Health Worker (CHW) certification, choose one that aligns with your career aspirations and fills a gap in your skill set. Each of these certifications can open doors to new opportunities and enhance your credibility in the field.

My Advice to Aspiring Public Health Consultants

Research, research, research! Public health consulting is unique, blending intricate public health knowledge with innovation and savvy business strategies. Understanding the depths of both these areas is crucial. So, before you leap, take a deep dive into understanding what this field entails.

Experience is your best teacher. Begin by soaking up as much experience as you can, whether through internships, volunteering, or even working within an established public health consulting firm. This isn't just about building your resume; it's about "getting your feet wet", gaining invaluable skills, and seeing if this path resonates with your passions and goals. You may think you want to do this work but until you do it, you really don't know.

Find your tribe. Connecting with others who share your aspirations and challenges can be incredibly enriching. Seek out those who've walked the path before you. Their insights, advice, and experiences are goldmines of information that can help you navigate your own journey. Plus, staying plugged into a community keeps you abreast of the latest trends and developments in the field.

Consider a mentor or coach. This journey is exhilarating for sure, but it can also be daunting without the right guidance. A coach who understands the public health and entrepreneurial landscape can be a Godsend, helping you develop the business acumen you might not have picked up in your public health studies. They can offer not just advice but also connections that are invaluable to you as you build your business venture.

Purposeful Partnerships
My ideal client is deeply committed to making a tangible difference in public health. They are leaders in public health organizations, healthcare systems, or community-based organizations who recognize the value of empowering their workforce, enhancing their leadership skills, and expanding their community impact. These clients are open to innovative, evidence-based strategies and are ready to invest in training programs that not only educate but also inspire and transform their teams and the communities they serve.

My favorite projects are those that allow me to blend my expertise in nursing and public health with my passion for education and empowerment. I thrive on creating and delivering training programs that are immediately applicable to the real world, offering practical skills that participants can use right away.

Potential clients can connect with me through my website, Umemba Health, or via Quisha Umemba Consulting. I'm also active on professional social media platforms like LinkedIn, where I share insights and engage with the broader public health community. For direct inquiries, email is the best way to reach me. I'm always excited to hear from organizations and individuals looking to make a positive impact in public health and am ready to explore how we can work together to achieve their goals.

For more information about Umemba Health LLC and the services we provide, connect by *visiting the website:* umembahealth.com or by emailing quisha@umembahealth.com.

For more information about Quisha Umemba Consulting, connect by visiting the website: quishaumemba.com or by emailing publichealthpreneur@gmail.com.

Chapter 5:
Breaking Down Barriers to Support Healthy Communities

Dr. Jovonni Spinner, CEO and Founder of Beacon Public Health and Maryland Healthcare Commissioner (appointed by the Wes-Moore administration) is an award-winning health equity strategist, thought leader, and TEDx speaker dedicated to advancing health equity across all stages of life through research, education, and community building. She believes health is a basic human right and uses her voice to support inclusive public health programs that support under-represented and historically marginalized communities. Her work has been dedicated towards dismantling systemic barriers by helping organizations and public health professionals deliver dynamic, equity-driven, culturally tailored public health programs that meet the health needs of underserved communities.

Her passion for helping organizations, communities, and public health professionals has guided her as she led multi-million dollar state and federal health equity programs, including the Diversity in Clinical Trials Initiative, Community Health Worker Health Disparities Initiative, and Virginia Vaccines for Children Program for the Food and Drug Administration, National Institutes of Health, and the state of Virginia. The programs have collectively reached millions of consumers to help them make better informed health decisions, obtain the services they need, and advocate for healthier communities in the pursuit of health equity.

Dr. Spinner is also a public health adjunct professor, serves on non-profit boards, and is active in her community creating programs to build the public health workforce and mentoring early-career professionals. Her research interests include understanding the social and cultural impact of living overweight and obese among Black women and examining the root causes of health inequities and solutions to address these inequities.

She has been honored by the National Minority Quality Forum, deBeaumont Foundation, Prince George's County Social Innovation Fund, and Emory Alumni Association as a leader in Public Health. She is an alumna of Virginia Commonwealth, Emory, and Morgan State Universities.

Business Website: www.beaconpublichealth.com
Business Facebook: Beacon Public Health
Business Instagram: @BeaconPublicHealth
LinkedIn:https://www.linkedin.com/in/jovonni-spinner-mph-ches/

Breaking Down Barriers to Support Healthy Communities

Dr. Jovonni Spinner

Everyone's Journey is Unique
I tell my mentees that their voyage to becoming a public health entrepreneur and business owner will ebb and flow. There will be times when you have no idea what you're doing or how you're going to reach your next milestone and others where everything falls into place. That's normal.

As entrepreneurs, we're advised to have a solid plan and put in the work, then your dreams will come true. While true for some, I would be remiss if I didn't acknowledge the systemic barriers Black women face in entrepreneurship. Racial and gender biases affect funding accessibility (e.g. business credit, venture capital, angel investors) and networking opportunities, hindering business scalability. Minority Business Development agency data reveal disparities in business credit allocation with owners of color less likely to be approved for business credit. Lack of representation further compounds challenges, with Black women often finding themselves isolated in entrepreneurial spaces. Oftentimes, the system is rigged against you. Nevertheless, *I encourage you to not be discouraged.*

Despite these obstacles, recognizing your strengths and seeking mentorship can help navigate through systemic hurdles.

We all want to reach our goals by the quickest and easiest path possible. But if you look back on most of your achievements, you will see that there were bumps and bruises along the way. The key is to learn and build your knowledge base as you go. My journey has been no different and continues to evolve, but it has been worth it because I've been pursuing my passion. To make the load lighter, take the pressure off yourself. Don't compare your abilities and achievements to those of others. You are your only competition.

When you focus on yourself and mind the business that pays you, you'll find less distractions and you'll move further and faster to your goal. Continue to stay in your lane and be your best YOU!

Finding my Purpose and Passion
Growing up in a Black household, my parents instilled in me the value of excellence and the importance of doing well in school. Education was my ticket to success, a means to achieve the life I dreamed of – a life of service and making a positive impact on my community. A life where I didn't have to struggle (financially, mentally, physically, or spiritually) and could use my privilege to advocate and support others who needed it most. They believed in my brilliance before I knew I had it.

Looking back, I realize how important mentorship was to help me figure out my career goals, instill confidence, and support my growth. In high school, my dental career teacher, Mrs. Williams, was instrumental in this. She believed in my ability and nurtured my skills, making me believe I could do great things. She encouraged me to participate in national dental competitions and gave me my first exposure to healthcare careers. This would later be repeated in undergrad. Shout out to my research professor, Kevin Jones, who really kept me engaged and honed my critical thinking skills that would later prove to be invaluable.

Undergrad was very challenging - not the whimsical experience I thought it was going to be. What started off as naïve enthusiasm and a can-do attitude led to me being at a crossroads, questioning my degree choice and suffering from burn-out. I wasn't alone in this and know this is the price you can pay for excellence. Between the late nights studying, holding down multiple jobs to survive, and just trying to figure out life—plus the 30-pound weight gain—I was tired. By the end, I was just happy to walk across the stage and get my degree. It wasn't all grim though. Even though I majored in Biology with intentions of a career in dentistry, after some soul searching and a few twists, I landed upon public health. And for that, I'm grateful.

My Shift in Focus

I dived into graduate-level courses to explore my interests while also working as an Analyst at a non-profit reviewing Medicaid claims for outpatient procedures. It was during a class on Public Health Issues in African-American Communities that a light-bulb-moment occurred. This was it! I quickly realized that what I was searching for was a way to help my community to be healthier without being a healthcare provider. By shifting my focus from individual work to community work, I could look at systemic barriers and figure out solutions for improving community health.

I went on to earn my Masters and Doctorate in Public Health and became a Certified Health Education Specialist. However, my path was not exactly linear. I took breaks after every degree and worked full-time the entire time. This worked for me because I could gain real life work experience, and when I went back to school for my advanced degrees, I was ready. I had a better perspective on how to manage work, school, and my personal life, and my support system was in place. I had effectively equipped myself to do well. Thank God for my can-do attitude, persistence, and tenacity, plus a healthy dose of curiosity and love of learning.

Health is a Basic Human Right

Fighting for health equity by addressing historical abuses and modern-day oppression was something I wanted to dig my heels into.

Growing up, I witnessed health inequities, but just didn't have the term to describe what I was seeing. My community was stuffed with fast food and liquor and there were corner stores on every block that sold little to no healthy food. Don't get me wrong, I loved going to the corner store after school and getting little snacks like fudge rounds and pickles wrapped in aluminum foil (fresh out of the jar of course!). When I got older, it was McDonald's fries and a sweet tea. Eventually, though, after hearing my family members talk, I pieced together the struggle of trying to manage chronic diseases, eat healthy, choosing between buying prescription medications or paying utility bills, getting to numerous doctors' appointments, managing childcare, being under-paid, living in substandard housing, and so many other issues that impacted their ability to achieve health equity – to live their best lives and thrive!

At the time, I was unaware that these challenges were identified as SDoH, contributing to health disparities resulting from inequities in healthcare access and resources. Through this, I realized I didn't have to wait for the "perfect" job to come along before I could make an impact. If you see that a community has a need and you have a solution, then start doing the work of interacting with the community. By the time I started my own business, this had become my "why", my mission - to work in positions that serve the most vulnerable communities, aligning my projects with my personal values and vision. It was Black Girl Magic in Action!

I have been blessed my entire public health career to have jobs that were aligned with my personal mission and vision. I remember my first "official" public health job at the Virginia Department of Health, Division of Immunization. I started off working as a consultant on the Virginia Vaccines for Children Program. In this role, I conducted quality assurance site visits for over 150 medical providers throughout the state, ensuring compliance with state and federal regulations for the Vaccines for Children program. I provided technical assistance, conducted medical chart reviews, interviewed providers, and prepared corrective action plans to improve compliance to make sure that children with Medicaid or who were uninsured or underinsured were able to receive their childhood vaccines. Shortly after starting, I was promoted to Supervisor and then Director where I managed a $20+ million federal grant, overseeing a team to ensure vaccine delivery, monitor quality assurance, and align program metrics with organizational goals, contributing to improved immunization services and fiscal responsibility.

Deciding that I had hit a glass ceiling and desiring to relocate, I decided to take a fellowship. This is where I pivoted and my next move might not have made sense to most. I went from being a director of a $20M program to a fellow (seems like a downgrade, right?). This is where I say sometimes you have to go left in order to go up (and advance). I relocated to Washington, DC to take an ORISE fellowship working with the National Vaccine Program Office to work on vaccine policy

Breaking Down Barriers to Support Healthy Communities

and finance issues. This was an opportunity to get a taste of the federal government and flex another public health muscle by working on policy issues - shifting from programming. I worked on initiatives to update the National Vaccine Plan by fostering partnerships across various sectors and conducted outreach to enhance influenza vaccination rates among healthcare personnel. Additionally, I provided support to the National Vaccine Advisory Committee to bolster public-private partnerships during the 2009 H1N1 outbreak and advocated for policy changes to improve vaccine reimbursement and accessibility. This job was a learning moment for me. I realized that I did not like working in policy. It was entirely too much gray space and I needed more tangible outcomes to make me feel purposeful in my work. Having this understanding of my desires led me to the National Institutes of Health (NIH)/National Heart, Lung, and Blood Institute.

Working at NIH was my first official federal job and you could not tell me anything. I was on fire! I landed a job as a Public Health Analyst working on the Community Health Worker Health Disparities Initiative which aims to help reduce health disparities in underserved and minority communities across the United States - with a focus on heart disease and asthma. When I first started, I managed the program evaluation. It was my job to make sense of the program data from pre and post-tests, training satisfaction surveys, etc. Eventually, my role grew and I ended up managing the entire $5 million dollar contract. I became a Certified Contracting Officer (similar to a Project Manager) and I oversaw the initiative to identify and implement culturally appropriate strategies to reduce cardiovascular disease and asthma disparities in under-served racial/ethnic communities and to independently plan, implement, monitor, and evaluate national public health education programs for cardiovascular disease, sickle cell disease, and asthma. One unique aspect of the program was establishing a partnership with the US. Department of Housing and Urban Development to work with local housing authorities to train residents to become community health workers which had never been done before.

I was sad to leave NIH, but with a reorganization and potential for the programs I was working on to be sunsetted, the writing was on the wall and it was time to find a new job. Fortunately, a new opportunity presented itself in an unsuspecting way. Out of all of the Department of Health and Human Services (HHS) agencies, I never in a million years wanted to work for the Food and Drug Administration. I heard that it was a hard place to work (code for work-life-home balance sucked) and working in a regulatory environment probably would not align with my core. However, a new opportunity presented itself under the Affordable Care Act of 2010. Every HHS agency was required to establish an Office of Minority Health (OMH). When I saw the posting for FDA's OMH position, in my mind, this was the perfect job for me and it turned out to be just that.

In my role as Associate Director for Outreach and Communications (promoted from Senior Public Health Advisor) at the Office of Minority Health and Health Equity, I led an award-winning national Outreach and Communication program, reaching 7+ million, engaging industry, academia (e.g. HBCUs, Minority-Serving Institutes), tribal entities, and other federal agencies. I served as an agency spokesperson on minority health, health equity, and health disparities issues. I provided expert guidance to SES-level Directors, Chief Scientist, and Commissioner on the implementation of laws regulating FDA's communication to minorities and increasing diversity in clinical trials; improved meaningful stakeholder engagement related to regulatory science; conducted outreach through multi-media campaigns, social media, lectures, and journal articles. I also spearheaded a training initiative to educate agency staff on diversity, bias, and cultural competency. During the COVID-19 pandemic, I also served on the Joint Information Center as the designated office lead to handle public information needs, with a specific focus on historically marginalized communities. This included meeting with stakeholder groups to educate and inform on the Agency's COVID-19 response efforts, create health education materials to dispel myths for the community and provide overall guidance to FDA on how to interact with diverse communities during this tumultuous and uncertain time.

Despite my very fulfilling journey of working in state and federal government public health positions, I started my career with an exit plan for entrepreneurship. Going into the federal government, I knew I wanted to work for one decade and then transition into starting my consulting firm. I probably would have stayed a bit longer in the government, but a few things accelerated my decision. The first being COVID-19. And secondly, the calling was becoming too great to ignore. You often hear that when God wants to make changes in your life, He makes you uncomfortable. He taps you on the shoulder to signal a change needs to happen and doors are going to open when you step out on faith. It was (and still is) scary and hard for me, but totally necessary. During that time, I had a professional coach, therapist, friends and family who all saw that my life was heading in a different direction and this was my moment to lean into my dream. Clearly, manifestation, meditation and prayer are powerful tools because I always said that when I turned 40, I was going to stop punching a clock and do my own thing. I wasn't exactly on that time frame, but not too far off either. I am a natural planner and adverse to risk, so it takes me a little longer to take action on some things – especially something as big as my career.

My Entrepreneurship Journey

Yes! I left my good government job. After working in state and federal public health positions, I decided to branch out and start my own company, Beacon Public Health. The mission of my company is to transform the health narrative for underserved communities through research, education, and community building. We're here to impact real change and address health inequities, a fundamental human right that should be accessible to everyone, regardless of their background.

Our projects are as dynamic and multi-faceted as the communities we serve. From capacity building, educating on chronic disease risk factors and promoting healthy lifestyles to designing, implementing, and evaluating sustainable public health programs, our work is rooted in authenticity and community engagement. We specialize in crafting culturally tailored health education communications that help individuals to make informed decisions. Our collaborative approach extends to supporting the public health workforce through professional development, ensuring they have the skills needed to make a lasting impact. Beacon's goal is to create partnerships with purpose, provide technical assistance to build organizational capacity, and address the pressing health needs of diverse communities. Together with our clients, we're rewriting the narrative, ensuring that every individual has the opportunity to live a healthy and whole life.

I've had the privilege of consulting for a diverse range of clients, mostly in the non-profit sector. Some of those clients include the Association of Black Cardiologists, the National

Association of City and County Health Officials, HealthCare Ready, Elevation Educational Consulting Group, and Feeding America, among others. While I pitched many of those clients or responded to requests for proposals, some of those contracts were secured because of my network (in the words of Jay-Z, "your network is your net worth"). Each organization shares our vision of building healthy and whole communities. Working with organizations I once aspired to join is a fulfilling full-circle experience, especially now as I provide consulting services, a highlight of my entrepreneurial journey.

One project that stands out is developing a series of professional development trainings for the National Association of City and County Health Officials (NACCHO) to train and support health department staff nationwide to build their capacity to address health equity amidst the COVID-19 pandemic by using the community health worker model. This project was particularly enticing because I was able to pull from my previous experience managing the Community Health Workers (CHW) Health Disparities Initiative at the National Institutes of Health, National Heart, Lung, and Blood Institute. I knew I had the skill sets and knowledge and it aligned with the mission of my company. This was a win-win for me.

Equity starts by engaging your audience. In this case, to ensure the CHW trainings were relevant, my team conducted a focus group with CHWs to better learn about their lived experiences and what their needs were to effectively do their job. From there, my team developed a series of trainings rooted in health equity to train local health department staff on how to create, build, manage, and sustain CHW programs. We made sure the trainings centered the voices of CHWs and had them participate in a panel discussion with staff members so they could fully realize how they positively impacted their community's health and the role they play as a part of the healthcare team. The trainings and educational materials developed had a positive impact on increasing the staff's ability to manage their CHW program.

Another project that I am proud of was working on NACCHO's well-known long-standing online public health resource course, Roots of Health Inequity. The public health history chapter in the course needed to be updated. We were given the liberty to really expand on the intersections of public health, the political challenges, the historical abuses and inequities that have persisted within our country, and to explicitly call out the injustices. Doing so helped elevate the module to be reflective of the current landscape and to work towards addressing health inequities. We had to hone in on our research, training, and communication skills to be able to adequately address the key topic areas and make it relevant for future trainees who would take the course. To be a part of a forward-thinking project that will be used for many years to come feels good and solidifies that I am on the right path.

Upsides and Downfalls of Entrepreneurship
Entrepreneurship is not for everyone, particularly the faint of heart. You must be ready to be responsible for your own and someone else's livelihood (their paycheck). You must examine your personal and company values and mission, consider your goals, the business' goals, your clients' goals, the needs of your staff, and all of the public scrutiny that comes with that. I don't say this to discourage you but to be realistic - unlike most messaging about entrepreneurship that makes it seem so easy. It may or may not be easy for you, but that's the reality and it's par for the course.

Every day is going to be different. Some days feel glamorous checking off my to do list and securing the bag and others seem like everything is falling apart. I want to scream at the top of my lungs and my tummy is bubbling from stress causing me to momentarily regret my path and wonder why I chose this life. The late nights trying to figure it out, completing that one task that should have taken ten minutes and now it's two hours later, wearing multiple hats, having a gazillion client meetings that still don't result in a contract. All while wondering, am I good enough to do this? Once I get off the pity pot, I remind myself that I am built for this, and I have the skills, knowledge, and passion to do the work and do it well. This life is not easy, but I'm happy with the path I've chosen, and I'm willing to take the good with the less than pleasant.

As an entrepreneur, you'll need to have enough discernment to know when to pivot and adjust your course. You need to understand that altering your plan does not make you a failure. We learn from failure, so embrace that. Doing so has made me a successful businesswoman.

Present day, I am more focused on strategy and growth, building client relationships and creating sustainable revenue streams. However, starting off, I did everything: accounting, social media, developing and implementing trainings, creating health education materials, planning and hosting webinars, and more. I was doing the most! I always had a vision to scale my company and now, wherever I can, I outsource and bring on consultants to support projects. I do this even when it means less profits for me because it is not sustainable for me to do everything long-term. Doing so will ultimately stunt growth and lead to burnout. I want to focus on doing a few things exceptionally well because mediocrity is not my thing. Public health may not always be financially lucrative, but when your purpose aligns with your mission, you can still make a good living while finding meaning and value in your work. I have been in public health for almost two decades, so I know good work, and now as a leader, it is time to let go (AKA "delegate" to all my Type A folks out there) and allow my team to take on tasks so I can focus on building the company.

The hardest thing to do as an entrepreneur is to transition from doing all the work to functioning as a CEO, which is why building a team of trusted partners and collaborators is so important. My brand is built on quality, so I have to surround myself with others who have the same mindset.

People always ask what I do every day. Given that we offer a mix of products and services, my day-to-day duties can look very different. Some days, I focus on strategy—mapping projects, aligning resources with our goals, managing projects, assessing progress, and refining our approach—to ensure the best product for our clients. Every day I am focused on building and supporting my team. As the CEO, I still create trainings, write articles, and manage the website, among other things. I also focus a good amount of time on mentoring early career professionals - helping them figure out their career and academic paths. Paying it forward is so important to me because, as a Black woman, I feel we need to support and promote each other. There is room enough for everyone at the table. Lord only knows how my trajectory might have changed if I knew then what I know now!

Even though my company has been successful in producing some amazing outcomes, there are challenges that impact just about every entrepreneur that I know (regardless of industry), including lack of resources, inadequate funding, and lack of value for our field.

COVID-19 shined a light on the fragmented healthcare system, the need for public health, and health inequities that have continued to persist for centuries. Public health was finally in the spotlight. Prior to COVID-19, most people could not differentiate between healthcare and public health and had no idea of our role to keep our communities safe and healthy.

Pay disparities are another challenge. Because of the limited resources and sometimes lack of perceived value placed on our work, some companies don't want to (or can't) pay an equitable rate. They want us to do more for less – adding on additional tasks – and because we want to appease the client and preserve the relationship, some consultants don't feel comfortable advocating for additional pay to cover the added requests. As consultants, we are often competing for the same work and in the process, we can undercut each other thus diminishing our financial value. While I firmly believe there is enough room for everyone to thrive and what's for me will be for me, I know that this is an issue that my colleagues and I often grapple with.

Another challenge is what I like to call a "microwave mentality". Some clients want everything done yesterday. They want work done before the contract is even signed. To mitigate this, I try to impose reasonable timelines and manage expectations while still maintaining a high level of quality - one of the cornerstones of my brand.

Staying Relevant in Evolving Times
Learning and engaging with others to stay relevant in today's changing climate is one strategy to keep my skills sharp. Staying on top of relevant trends and applying them to your business practices is vital. This is part of my commitment to excellence. I am a sucker for a webinar or training that will

help me learn about new topics, dig deeper into things I already know about, or just have an opportunity to convene with others in the public health space. Networking is important to hear about what others are doing and to learn about emerging trends and innovative practices. Truthfully, it can get lonely as an entrepreneur because some days it is just you and all of your big ideas!

You will need to master the core competencies of public health, as well as the soft skills: the art of communication and negotiation, being nimble and adaptable, and being culturally competent. These skills will take you just as far as knowing how to use the correct statistical test to perform your data analysis or the right theory to use to design your program.

When I first started working in government, a colleague told me that I would do well in my career because of my personality - my ability to relate to people, authentically engage them, and meet them at their place of need. My diplomatic nature and ability to communicate in a clear and transparent manner has gotten me far. I strongly believe that the foundation of a good client relationship is listening and understanding what their needs are and figuring out if you can meet those needs. I have no problem turning down a client when we are not aligned because all money ain't good money. I take a collaborative approach so the client understands what will happen every step of the way, which helps them build trust in my abilities. You also need to provide value to show them why they should hire you. What can you bring to the table that no one else can? What is your value proposition?

Anyone interested in becoming a public health consultant should consider becoming a Certified Health Education Specialist or becoming Certified in Public Health. You should also consider trainings and certifications that help fill a gap in your skill set or may complement your work - project management, business development, grant writing, data analysis, or specific certifications in topics related to your niche. Always stay in the growth mindset and be willing to learn, adapt, and pivot.

I get my news from reputable sources like NPR and CNN, subscribe to different public health news feeds and podcasts, and read literature. I follow trustworthy public health experts, organizations, and institutions on social media. My knowledge and reputation are my currency, so I must remain current, relevant, and aligned with the dynamic nature of public health. This commitment not only enhances my expertise but also allows me to contribute meaningfully to the advancement of health equity and community well-being.

Emerging Trends in Public Health
Regardless of your niche, you have to embrace data and evidence. Data-driven decision-making will reshape consulting strategies, requiring professionals to enhance their proficiency in data analytics, interpretation, and implementation of technology-driven solutions. The evolving landscape also calls for a proactive approach to public health policy and advocacy. Consultants must stay informed about policy changes and contribute to shaping equitable health policies. As public health continues to intersect with diverse fields, interdisciplinary collaboration with experts from various domains becomes crucial. Technology is going to continue to transform how we think and do our work. Staying technologically savvy, embracing personalized approaches, and prioritizing health equity will be critical areas for public health consultants to focus on. Here is my take on a few emerging trends.

Artificial Intelligence: I believe artificial intelligence (AI) is here to stay. As public health leaders, we must begin to decide what that impact will look like – before others decide for us. Its impact is already evident in areas such as predictive analytics, personalized medicine, and efficient data management, offering unprecedented opportunities to enhance public health outcomes and address systemic disparities. For example, AI may be used to identify patterns in large datasets or to identify behavioral patterns that can be used to tailor public health interventions. As we navigate the future, AI is poised to become an even more influential force, empowering public health practitioners with innovative tools and insights for more effective and equitable healthcare solutions. However, with any innovation, we must be careful to manage the ethics surrounding AI using similar standards to how we conduct all research studies. We must be careful to use the tools appropriately and ethically, safeguard individual privacy, ensure equity, and maintain transparency.

Digital Health: One significant trend is the increasing focus on digital health solutions, leveraging technology for data analytics, telehealth, and health informatics. Public health professionals should enhance their digital literacy and adaptability to leverage these tools effectively. In the process, we can't forget about communities with lower digital literacy. The digital divide can exacerbate existing health disparities, so it is important that public health supports the digital literacy needed for communities to navigate the healthcare system.

Community Centric Approaches: The growing recognition of the SDoH is steering consulting towards holistic, community-centered approaches. We have to move past a one-size-fits-all approach because it simply does not work. Programs, resources, and policies need to be tailored for each community that centers their voice and their needs. Professionals should hone their skills in community engagement, cultural competency, and collaborative partnerships to address the root causes of health inequities. Public health organizations and companies should invest in culturally diverse staff to support authentic community-centric approaches.

It's on my radar constantly, but an emphasis on health equity and justice will likely intensify, demanding consultants integrate equity frameworks into their strategies. This will drive the transformation necessary to achieve health equity and justice.

Best Practices
Recognizing that the community holds invaluable expertise, my approach to developing and implementing effective public health strategies for diverse communities is rooted in community engagement and collaboration. I initiate the process by actively listening to community members, understanding their unique needs, and respecting cultural norms. Once I have a solid understanding of the community's needs, I make sure that interventions and programs are culturally tailored, relevant, and reflective of the community's priorities, and most importantly, include the community in decision making.

Here is an example of how we put best practices into action. We launched the **Mamas 4 Life** maternal education campaign (www.beaconpublichealth.com/mamas4life) to raise awareness about the role of doulas and midwives. I centered the voices of mothers who had used a doula and/or midwife by asking them to share their lived experience. I talked to doulas and midwives to understand their work. I used all that information to inform the campaign which resulted in a webinar, toolkit and other resources. The webinar lifted up the voices of doulas and midwives while they spoke directly to the communities of families who needed to hear from loving caring maternal health practitioners. I also created social media graphics that shared the mother's quotes and images of their birth or with their children. All of this normalized the conversation and made it relatable to others. When people see themselves in the materials and programs, they are more likely to spur positive behavioral change. This collaborative approach not only enhances the effectiveness of public health strategies but also fosters a sense of ownership and empowerment within the communities I serve.

For all of BPH's campaigns, I make sure to use clear language free of jargon, using images that reflect the positive aspects of the community, and align the materials with the intended purpose. I make sure to meet people at their place of need. For example, if I know a certain community is using social media, then I develop health education tools for social media. If I know they value print materials, then I make sure the materials are tailored for printing and downloading. I also like to call on members of the community to help review materials before launch.

Preserving Your Sanity: Maintaining the Proverbial Work-Life Balance

You must find out what works best for you to maintain balance. There is always going to be something on your "To-Do" list, so you have to figure out how to prioritize and ensure your mental, physical, and spiritual health are in order. Being intentional about my self-care and focusing on things that bring me joy, even though it is hard at times, is important. I continually reassess and adapt to counterbalance managing all aspects of my life. Not only am I a business owner, but I am also a daughter, sister, friend and many other roles. I volunteer and serve on numerous boards and recently was appointed to be a Maryland Healthcare Commissioner. Plus, I enjoy time with MYSELF.

To maintain balance, I incorporate checks and balances to keep me on track. While many things are important, not everything is a priority. And let's be real, I am not saving lives. Most of the projects I work on, no one has asked for, so if I need to alter the deadline for the next health education campaign so I don't run myself into the ground, then that is perfectly fine with me.

These are my ground rules.

No Computer in the Bedroom:
This is just setting myself up to work the night away disrupting my peace and relaxation.

Set Work Hours:
I usually work no later than 8 pm. I get up, close the office door, and in theory, never look back until the next morning. Doing so allows me time to unwind before bedtime.

Do Not Disturb:
When bedtime comes, my phone automatically goes into "Do Not Disturb" mode to avoid constant notifications sucking me into more screen time. Now this doesn't mean that my mind automatically shuts down, but it is a good

practice to simulate balance. I also use the Do Not Disturb feature when I need to focus on a task.

Say No:
Learning how to say no and not feel guilty is a skill I have been honing for a few years now. It's tough when you have an inherent nature to be helpful, but also stems from dealing with perfectionism and people-pleasing. Just remember, every battle is not yours to fight or fix.

Take Naps (and breaks):
I am a proud member of the nap ministry! Sometimes, when I curl up to get cozy for naptime in my comfy green chair in my office and hear my email notification or text message, I tell my brain that whatever it is, it can wait. Taking time for my nap allows me to be rested and fully alert to tackle anything when I wake up.

The "Say Yes" Checklist:
Recently, I created a checklist to help me decide if I am going to take on another project.
1. Does it bring me joy?
2. Does it align with my purpose?
3. Does it help me grow professionally or personally?
4. Does it generate adequate revenue (proportional to the amount of effort needed)?
5. Most importantly, what do I have to say no to to take on this project? What will I have to sacrifice to take on this project: sleep or working out, hanging out with my family, missing an important event, or risking my

reputation by overpromising and potentially under delivering.

Using this checklist has been key to help me not take on too much. Everything can appear to be a good opportunity, but sometimes you just have to say no.

Self-care:
We all know you can't pour from an empty cup, so self-care is necessary. Take time to indulge in services like massages and stretch therapy sessions. Take much needed vacations, go out with friends or family, or just sit in the house and binge watch a good show on TV to decompress. Walking and breathing in the fresh air, looking at nature, and taking time to meditate are helpful too. Nature has a unique energy that you will absorb. It can center and balance you. Do what brings you joy.

Don't underestimate the power of gratitude. Being thankful for all my many successes and the so-called "failures" gives me a healthy perspective and keeps me centered and grounded, all of which go in my journal and gratitude box. Oh, and having a phenomenal therapist helps keep me on track.

Final Thoughts
I am proud and amazed at my journey. While this only represents a snippet, I want to encourage other entrepreneurs to follow your dreams. Stop ruminating and just try. You can continually refine your services and products, but you will never know how to refine them if you don't get started. While you are developing your plan, think about what competencies you need to master, who you

need to have on your team, and what success looks like for you. Bottom line, you need to stay informed, keep your skills sharp, remain nimble and adaptable, and stay committed to addressing the evolving needs of the communities you serve. Another thing that has been helpful to me is building my personal board of directors. This consists of a financial advisor, tax advisor, lawyer, mentors, and sponsors who can help guide my path. Start small and build. That's the key.

Figure out your niche and find a good mentor and sponsor. A mentor will guide you in developing your vision, set goals and identify resources. A sponsor will speak up on your behalf when you are not in the room. They will recommend you for jobs, sing your praises, ensure that you are in the right places and meeting the right people. Both are great, but you also have to believe in yourself. Don't overthink it. If you have a great idea, don't get stuck in the planning phase. Striving for perfection will leave you with decision paralysis and you will never launch your idea. You can only refine something and make it better once you actually launch your product or service. Never promise a client more than you can handle, so always under promise and over deliver to avoid losing credibility and trust.

I've learned to celebrate my successes no matter how big or small, believe in myself and lean into my expertise and intuition, and stay mission focused. Your values will be the anchor that guides your decisions and your mission will be the beacon that guides you forward.

What's Next for Beacon Public Health

Beacon Public Health thrives when we work collaboratively with organizations who are committed to championing health equity through research, education, and community building. Our sweet spot lies in projects that focus on health education and professional development, and I will be looking to do more of this moving forward. We will be focused on topics crucial to our communities' well-being to support informed decision making and uplifting the public health profession through workforce development.

If you're ready to embark on a transformative journey toward health equity, I invite you to connect with us via email or social media. You can also visit our website at **www.beaconpublichealth.com** to schedule a discovery call where we can explore how our expertise aligns with your vision and how, together, we can create meaningful change in the pursuit of health equity.

Acknowledgements: Gratitude is one thing that keeps me going. I am grateful to everyone who has contributed to my journey, no matter how big or small. Thank you to my parents for instilling in me the value of education and a spirit of excellence. To my friends and family who have lent a listening ear for me to brainstorm ideas, providing support for me to build and grow my business, and have been my constant cheerleaders, always reminding me of my greatness...thank you! I am also grateful for my mentors and sponsors who have helped to usher me through my career and continued to support me at every phase. I am blessed beyond measure because of all of you.

Chapter 6:
Bridging My Life's Purpose to Profit

Jometra Hawkins-Sneed is often called a "community health translator" with life experience as a person who lives with Lupus. Jometra has served as a bridge between communities and policymakers, uncovering and communicating the needs of residents in underserved communities while advocating for policies that will help lift their socioeconomic status. She currently serves as the Chief Executive Officer of her health and racial equity consulting firm, Equity Bridge LLC ™, where she works with nonprofits, government agencies, healthcare systems, educational institutions and communities to build strategic plans that invest in the betterment of the community through equitable and healthy solutions. Prior to her business venture, Jometra attended Texas Southern University, where she studied Education. She has overseen key public health initiatives in Houston and surrounding areas and currently serves as the co-chair of the African American Health Coalition. She is also a former co-chair of the Acres Homes Health Action team, which was created as part of the City of Houston's Complete Communities Initiative. She currently serves as Assistant Presiding Officer and a Board Member for the Texas Department of State Health Services, Community Health Workers Advisory Committee. She holds the official titles of Community Health Worker, Board Co-Chair, Community Leader and now Author.

Business Website: equitybridgellc.com
Business Facebook: Equity Bridge llc
Business Instagram: @EquityBridgeLLC
LinkedIn: https://www.linkedin.com/company/equity-bridge-llc-a-jometra-hawkins-company/

Bridging My Life's Purpose to Profit
Jometra Hawkins-Sneed

Humble Beginnings
Growing up, I didn't know what I wanted to be, what I wanted to do or where I wanted to work. All I knew, from living in Galveston, Texas, is that I did not want to work in the hospital or in hospitality all my life. Considering that, I simply followed what I saw. I didn't have the ideal role model to help me explore various career opportunities. I only had my mom, my sister, my grandmother, a few teachers and God. Quickly, with limited options, I decided I wanted to be a teacher. They seemed to be financially stable with a place to live, a car, an ideal job that wasn't going anywhere and they got to work with kids (like me) every day.

I graduated high school within the top 10% of my class and just knew that would automatically make me successful. In 1999, I moved to Houston, Texas to pursue my Bachelors of Education at Texas Southern University. I quickly learned that college was harder than I could ever imagine, especially after having my first child in 2000. I continued my studies, but knew I had to find a job to pay bills, childcare costs and day-to-day living expenses. Thankfully, with so many family resources, I was able to continue college and get my first job in college as a Research Lab Technician at Baylor College of Medicine. This is where I fell in love with medical theory and helping people. Not quite public health but research. It was fascinating to see how my little job of picking DNA plaques, isolating DNA cells from a petri dish to perform a Plaque Assay, would turn into research on generating the first sequence of the human genome. This provided fundamental information about the human blueprint, which has since accelerated the study of human biology and improved the practice of medicine. Wow, what a difference I could make to millions of people, if I concentrated on health.

Finding My Footing

This realization led me to my next opportunity, Executive Assistant to the Executive Director of A Caring Safe Place, a transitional living facility for HIV positive men dealing with addiction. This opened my eyes to the world of public health education and really helping people one-on-one and in a group setting. The position was only a volunteer job where I collected a weekly wage of $50 to help transport myself to school and work, but this was the information, the education, the on-the-job training that I needed. It allowed me to be the secretary and file papers (my real job) and also learn public health education simultaneously. I knew what SDoH were before it was a term, because I saw it and lived it every day.

Because I had gained teaching experience in my volunteer position, I was able to get a temporary job as an Administrative Associate (AA) at the American Heart Association (AHA). Initially, this job was only to last six weeks. They just needed help wrapping up an event since the previous AA had moved on from the organization. However, those six weeks turned into 11 years, five promotions and too many employee awards to count. I transitioned from AA of Events in a small market to General AA, to Health Equity Specialist to Health Equity Director, to Sr. Health Equity Director to Sr. Director of Check. Change. Control for the Southwest Affiliate region and finally, Sr. Director of Community Impact & Healthcare Systems for the Houston Metropolitan area. I was truly a public health professional now with more than 13 years of experience after my tenure at the AHA.

My journey wasn't quite finished because I needed to explore more public health opportunities and spread my wings to learn more so I could give back more. As a result, I transitioned into an opportunity at Baker Ripley as the Community Developer, managing the newest and largest community center in the Houston area, The East Aldine Campus. There, I learned how to work with staff, uncover, rediscover and develop resources needed in the community. From the SDoH, Rental Assistance, Winter Storm assistance, daily educational and life skill classes, I had the opportunity to do great things for some amazing neighbors in that region. But, I couldn't stop there. To be the ultimate public health professional, I had to learn more about government public health and how the community could take advantage of the resources from the government agencies and other nonprofits. So I decided to take a leap of faith and joined the Harris County Public Health team as a FUSE Corp. Executive Fellow, working directly with the COVID Division Director on Equity. What a challenge this was! Just navigating the COVID years alone was hard, but working in a division that supported COVID vaccines, outreach and initiatives was even harder, especially in a government setting with so many restrictions on what to do and how to do it. This is where I found my passion for consulting. This is where I knew my professional experience, lived experience and education would take me to a new level. I was a valuable asset with my community engagement knowledge, my public health education and my character of wanting to help so many. This fellowship showed me that I could be a Public Health Entrepreneur. I became the consultant for many in that space as an Executive Fellow. I knew my stuff and others knew it too. They leaned into my knowledge and allowed me to create amazing policies and programs like "The Equity First Initiative", where equity is not an afterthought but intertwined in the initiative from conception. Also, the Vaccine Partner Incentive Program (VPIP), where we connected and compensated trusted community partners that helped HCPH serve thousands of Harris County residents with COVID vaccines and an incentive of $100 because we knew there were SDoH barriers like transportation, time off work, daycare issues and more that prevented people from getting the vaccine. This was a national model that garnered lots of federal attention and served our region well. Developing programs that were equitable and targeted to reach the right demographic that needed the resources and services the most was truly my calling and my passion. It was like the heavens opened and God walked out and said "YOU FOUND IT!"

During my time at HCPH, I filed for my business name and LLC under Equity Bridge, because I knew that I could be a consultant to *bridge* the gap between employees and employer, government and community and use my purpose to make profit.

Stepping Into My Purpose

After my tenure as an Executive Fellow for FUSE Corp at Harris County Public Health, I started reaching out to friends and colleagues of the past to feel out the industry and find my first contract. To my surprise, it came quicker than I could have imagined. A good friend, Tony Salah of Heka Health, a health and wellness technology company, reached out and inquired about my new business and the services I offered. Of course I was excited, grateful and amazed at how God continued to sustain me. Tony informed me he had a part-time role available as Director of Account Management. This role allowed me to work with corporate employers, nonprofits, government agencies and so many more to develop engaging ways to stay healthy through blood pressure initiatives, walking challenges and employee wellness interventions. It allowed me to meet so many amazing people and travel the country while spreading health equity and public health initiatives in the form of fun activities. I was still interested in community health work and engaging with the community, so I continued to seek other opportunities to serve. Tony asked me to speak to an old friend that I worked with over 10 years ago at the AHA because he felt it was beneficial for us to reconnect. Little did I know, the old friend needed my help on a community health workers' initiative at a major hospital system in Michigan. Of course I knew about community health workers because I was passionate about their work, had been a board member on a Community Health Workers' Association and had been certified as a CHW years ago. It's funny how my passion project became my most lucrative consulting contract to date. In the midst of that, I accrued a contract with a few higher education institutions like Texas Southern University, University of Texas Medical Branch Galveston, a featured professor opportunity at Rice University, Glasscock School of Continuing Studies and a volunteer consultant and member of the University of Texas Houston Health Science Center, School of Public Health, Health Equity Collective, CHW Network. Wow, I had made it to a place where I had a full-time role as a public health consultant and entrepreneur.

As my client list grew, my day-to-day activities also expanded. The great thing about owning your own company is the ability to work on your own time. I set my own schedule that's convenient for me, so of course my hours are Monday - Friday, 9 am-4 pm. I am available earlier or later on a rare occasion because in the words of Tabitha Brown, "That's my Business!" I will say, without my multiple calendars (personal, professional, volunteer and kids), Google Drive and multiple devices, I would be lost. I keep a meticulous calendar because if it's not on my calendar, it doesn't exist. Each evening, I check my calendar to see what the next day will bring, set up my home office, schedule my alarm and prepare for the day. Many days are filled with conference calls to develop strategies, talk through projects, evaluate progress and learn. I definitely schedule lots of learning sessions to stay up to date on what's happening in the community as it relates to health, equity and healthcare as a whole. I often find specific topics that interest me or topics that might have been mentioned in previous conversations so I become a great resource for new information.

Challenges Faced

In my opinion, being a small business in a large city sometimes brings a challenge. That's why I stay up to date on the latest information, attend the appropriate events and continue to build my network. It's a fine art in Houston, knowing where to find resources and discovering the right connections that just might need my services and my skill set. Other common challenges that are faced by public health consultants are navigating the conversation around expectations as a consultant with a specific scope of work. Often, we want to do the best job to continue serving the client or get referrals for doing such a great job, which sometimes leads to being roped into providing services that are not necessarily a part of your intended scope. It's a fine line in being a great consultant that goes above and beyond for the client and staying the course of the intended scope. Crossing that line gets you way off your intended deliverables and often pushes back the timeline of your project completion.

Visibility-Credibility-Profitability

As a consultant in any industry, it's important to stay educated in your field of study. I often chat with previous colleagues about their current work. I'll schedule time for lunch or coffee as a friendly hello and business meeting to discuss potential events, education, common trends and community engagement opportunities to keep a pulse on the industry. I am also a busy body and love to network. Many times, I'll find meetups, professional gatherings, education sessions and nonprofit, government or institutional collaboratives that discuss current agendas, policies and health equity initiatives. I also volunteer for many organizations to stay on top of what the community has to say, what the industry trends are and who the major players could be.

One of my volunteer initiatives, specifically, is as the Co-Chair and Executive Director of The African American Health Coalition, which allows me to partner with all the public health agencies from government, corporations, nonprofits, community-based and faith-based organizations. In this role, I provide volunteer consulting, strategic planning and community engagement activities to build trusted relationships and strategic alliances in the community that once again fuels my passion and helps me to continue to grow as a public health professional. I try to stay connected to the industry as much as possible. I am also the Assistant Presiding Officer and Workforce Subcommittee Chair for the Department of State Health Services CHW Promotor(a)s Advisory Committee & Board. I volunteer my time to advocate for CHWs while gaining knowledge of the system, policies and advances on the state and national level. Attending community events, health professional gatherings, educational sessions and networking is a must. Recently, I attended the ForbesBLK summit in Atlanta, GA to network and learn from those business leaders who have paved the way and continue to thrive. While there, I met so many amazing people who worked for companies that could use my expertise while listening to a panel of business leaders from Microsoft, Amazon, Netflix, Forbes and so many more.

Public Health Trends
I foresee many trends shifting in the future of public health consulting. Because health equity is my wheelhouse, many policies, mandates, bills and laws are moving away from Diversity, Equity and Inclusion in title. With this shift, it is so important to stay the course and include all these attributes so these values, goals and objectives stay centered around equity. Even if it's not in title, equity should be ingrained in the processes, policies and programs to be more inclusive and create diverse opportunities for all. If my work helps my clients to continue to consider DEI as a very important piece from the start of any strategy, my work is impactful. I believe we should all stay diligent in our public health work as it relates to DEI and continue to push past the trend to create sustainable

methods for DEI. That means, not just adding those words, but including the actions from concept.

Bridging the Gap

When approaching development and implementation of effective public health strategies for diverse communities, I always start with the client and the community. I have a motto that I tell every one of my clients: To be effective, you MUST give the community what they have asked for, not just what you have. So many times organizations come up with their own methods and strategies to change the world without asking the world what needs to be changed or the method that would work best to solve issues in the community. Public Health Officials garner support from federal and state governments only to fail at the community level because no one considered the community's wants and needs. A landscape analysis is always a great start to be effective. Survey your target population, the community, employees, community partners, nonprofits, community-based organizations and faith-based organizations to get their perspective before launching a program for that audience. If you have resources, find out who needs them the most and cater to that population. Gather support from your client to find collaborative partners that either serve this population or have connections to reach these populations.

Recently, I came across a specific project where my expertise as a consultant made a significant impact on public health outcomes. I was asked to be a community ambassador and consultant for a research study that discussed Social Responsibility in Research focused on Maternal Health, Mental Health/Substance Abuse and HIV/Aids. The project scope required me to participate in facilitated discussions where my role was to develop a recruitment strategy for community engagement, translate the community perspective to the larger group and help to evaluate the outcomes of the community response. Through this study, we found many health equity issues that bubbled to the top as well as many barriers to provide education, awareness and effective communication. Researchers normally do their research and focus on the topics without a consideration of the social responsibility they have to the targeted audience, the community as a whole and the research study participants. My involvement helped to open their eyes to the many barriers to effective implementation of research or best practices, the lack of communication and education given to the people that need it the most, as well as the issues with access, innovation and education around the specific focus areas. With my community translations, effective communication and lived experience, I helped create a renewed mindset as it relates to informing, including and involving community members in research at a more intense level.

Sharing the expertise with the research study was just one successful and memorable consulting experience I've had. There have been many other moments of "aha" that have made the client and myself very successful in our endeavors. One of the most memorable experiences I've been a part of is the AIM project, Assess, Implement and Mobilize, at Texas Southern University, where we wanted to discover what was the health status and current help needs in the Third Ward community of Houston, TX. My role in this project was to facilitate community focus groups, create community engagement strategies, build trusted community partnerships and engage community stakeholders at events. This opportunity really allowed me to use every tool in the book as it relates to community engagement. Texas Southern is in the heart of Third Ward but is often its own community. This was a very important project to not only *bridge* the gap between community and the institution, but to also allow for health equity and community intervention to clash and make beautiful music.

The AIM project opened so many doors to community collaborations, resource navigation, uncovering and rediscovering resources and tools that were underutilized and forgotten. Now this was not an easy thing to do. Many partners and community members were apprehensive of the intentions of the institution and building trust was a huge hurdle. With the collaboration and dedication of an entire community, including city government, higher education institutions, local nonprofits, social services agencies, community leaders and so many others, we were able to build the strong connections needed to have a successful experience. This community is better for the continued work of the institution, its partner alignments and commitments to the health equity of Third Ward.

Work-Life Balance
Maintaining a work-life balance has been very easy, yet difficult, at the same time for me. I made a promise to my husband and kids that I'd make time for them, my health, and myself while building a lucrative business. I say easy because I create my own schedule. I work on what I'm passionate about and I do what makes good business sense. This can also be overwhelming and hard to manage when I take on too much too fast. There are so many great passion projects, consulting and government contracts that are available for small businesses that sometimes I get in over my head managing these alone. Good thing I have friends, previous colleagues and business relationships that are willing to help pull some of the weight as a 1099 contract employee or volunteer. To incorporate that balance, I also schedule mini vacations with my kids and spouse when traveling for work. Bleasure, a mix of business and pleasure, has become my ultimate word of the century. If I have an opportunity to bring my family, make money and stay an extra couple of days, I'm going to make the best out of it.

Skills & Competencies for Success
While work-life balance is a must, it should also be considered a critical competency a public health consultant should possess. Other competencies that are crucial for the public health entrepreneur are problem solving skills, analytical skills, innovation, interpersonal skills, communication, emotional intelligence, collaboration, practical thinking and so much more. These particular competencies are held high on my list as consultants should lead the way to better solutions. Our core competencies should roll over into the work we do. It's important to hold these things close to the work we do because it's what separates us from the rest. Holding true to these values allows for brand recognition, credibility and sustainability because you are trusted, tried and true.

Never Stop Learning
There are many trainings and education available for public health professionals that are very beneficial for consultants as well. Many government agencies and nonprofits offer free and low cost training that would definitely add value to the work we do. A few training categories I would recommend are: leadership, emotional intelligence, building sustainable relationships and also any government contract consulting training. There are so many opportunities to attain a contract when you know what to do and how to do it from the major sources, so stay on top of those opportunities.

My Greatest Piece of Advice
While relationships are key to sustaining any business, I would advise anyone interested in public health consulting to never stop building relationships. Continue to network, engage and speak up. Sometimes we are in settings where knowledge is valuable, but because we don't speak up or add value to the conversation, we are overlooked for opportunities to serve in a major capacity. I'd also say, volunteer! This work that I do is my passion. Of course I make great money helping others build their business or program, but there's nothing like

advancing a cause because it's important to you. Last year, I decided to chair the Walk to End Lupus at Texas Southern University and raise awareness of an autoimmune disease that had taken over my life. Because I was passionate and adamant about finding a cure or better ways to treat the disease, I put my hands, feet and wallet into action. My work was not in vain because thousands of people came out to walk for the cause, we raised lots of money to benefit the Lupus Foundation of America Texas Gulf Coast Chapter and so many Lupus Warriors stepped up to talk about their diagnosis to create more awareness of the disease. Passion met purpose and allowed me to be featured on so many media platforms, which in turn, helped boost business because I was a thriving Lupus Warrior continuing to follow my dreams despite my health challenges.

My Ideal Client

My ideal clients span a wide range of industries. My skill sets and consulting offerings can nearly service any industry that works directly with people. I particularly like to serve in strategic planning and concept building to innovate and create amazing opportunities in public health. I've worked with health nonprofits, government public health agencies, community and faith-based organizations as well as corporate employee engagement teams. My most favorite projects to work on are Community Health Worker employer programs, Community Engagement initiatives and creating innovative health programming. I've thrived my entire career building fun, impactful and creative strategies to reach minority communities. It's my passion for BiPoC communities to have equitable opportunities and access to resources, ultimately creating more diversity in the program offerings and engagement innovation.

Because my reputation precedes me, particularly my accomplishments in building blood pressure initiatives and community engagement strategies, opportunities to work directly with my ideal clients have arisen. Through my expertise and experience, I've secured a collaborative partnership with Yale, Methodist Hospital Houston, The African American Male Wellness Agency and Boston General on a four-year blood pressure control research study. Look how far I've come!

All in all, being a public health entrepreneur is hard work. You must put in lots of time building your strategy, being very clear on your services, solidifying what you can provide, and being organized and time conscientious. If you're operating in your passion and being very persistent about the goals you want to achieve, inevitably, that passion will lead to profit. Just be sure to budget well to maintain the profit!

For more information about Equity Bridge LLC, our CEO, Jometra Hawkins-Sneed, and the services we provide, connect with us by visiting our website: equitybridgellc.com, or by emailing: jo@equitybridgellc.com or contact us by phone at (530) 712-4278.

Acknowledgements: I would like to thank God for allowing me to explore my wildest dreams of becoming an author, an entrepreneur and for sustaining my business over the last few years. I'd also like to thank my mom, Diane Lyons, my sister, Dimetra Lyons-Wise, and my children, Daniel, Destiny, Demyan, Diamond and Dashaun Pinesette, for allowing me the space to explore with no doubt that their mom can do anything. I'd also like to thank my husbae, Lester Sneed, for supporting me no matter what. Through the eight months of building and uncertainty, he saw something in me and trusted the vision. I appreciate him more than he'll ever know. Big shout out to my friends and colleagues, Shante Fenner and Shalonda Tucker, for listening and helping me talk through my experiences included in this book as a professional and first-time author. I'd also like to thank Tony Salah, Dr. Willie Lawrence, the Corewell Health South team, Zuri Dale at Texas Southern University and all my clients who trusted me to engage with your staff, be a thought leader, connector and advocate within those organizations. To our Editor and Publisher, Whitney Brooks, all I can say is: You did that! I literally asked God on a Tuesday to allow me to write a book and by Thursday the opportunity had arrived. Thank you Quisha Umemba, our Visionary Author, for following the voice of Him and allowing me to be a part of a story-telling, historical and knowledge-gap filling piece of educational literature infused with successful life experiences. And to any and everyone who's supported me past, present, or in the future, thank you for your unwavering and continuous support. It means the world to me!

XOXO, Jo...

Chapter 7:
Taking Action Beyond Data Insights

Vanessa Da Costa is a public health entrepreneur and data consultant. She is British-born, American-bred, and of Zambian, Ghanaian, and Gambian descent. She is the Founder, CEO, and Principal Consultant of Chilombo Consulting, LLC. Chilombo Consulting provides human and equity-centered data strategy, collection, cleaning, analysis, visualization, and evaluation services to organizations looking to make sense of their quantitative and qualitative data. Her primary interest is in collaborating to promote data transparency, literacy, storytelling, and use in the areas of public health, workforce development, and education. Her experience includes working as a Data Analysis Advisor (Contractor) at the U.S. Agency for International Development (USAID) and as an Epidemiology Fellow at the Centers for Disease Control and Prevention (CDC) in South Africa. In these roles, she led data analysis, visualization, and strategic data communication deliverables for President's Emergency Plan for AIDS Relief (PEPFAR)-funded programs globally. She also served as a Peace Corps Community Health Volunteer and Graduate Research Assistant in Rwanda, and in research roles at the Georgia Emerging Infections Program, Duke Global Health Institute, RTI International, and the UNC Cecil G. Sheps Center for Health Services Research.

Vanessa offers speaking engagements at the intersection of public health career development and data skills training. She's held presentations and workshops for different organizations including the American Public Health Association, the Association of Black Researchers, and the Harvard T.H. Chan School of Public Health. Vanessa graduated from Emory University Rollins School of Public Health with a Master of Public Health (MPH) in Global

Epidemiology and from the University of North Carolina at Chapel Hill with a Bachelor of Science (BS) in Psychology and a minor in African Studies. Outside of her professional endeavors, Vanessa enjoys traveling, reading, and trying new restaurants. More information about Vanessa can be found at https://vanessadacosta.com.

Email: hello@chilomboconsulting.com
Business Website: https://chilomboconsulting.com
Business Instagram:
https://www.instagram.com/chilomboconsulting
LinkedIn: www.linkedin.com/in/vcdacosta
Business LinkedIn:
https://www.linkedin.com/company/chilomboconsulting

Taking Action Beyond Data Insights
Vanessa Da Costa

Laying the Foundation
From research to programs to consulting, my public health journey has taken me around the world and back! My career intention at the age of 17 was to become a pediatrician. After my first year in college, I decided to leave pre-medicine behind and instead explore health-related courses that went beyond the Biology and Chemistry courses needed for the pre-medicine track. I loved the courses I was able to take while at UNC-Chapel Hill that exposed me to Public Health. I took AIDS: Principles and Policies, Global Health Anthropology, Global Health Policy, and Health Policy and Management: U.S. Healthcare System. To further explore my newfound interest in Public Health, I became involved in a student organization, the Foundation for International Medical Relief of Children (FIMRC) and served as their Fundraising Chair. This opportunity exposed me to community-based service in Costa Rica. Although this experience positively influenced my interest in global health, in full transparency, it also introduced me to the negative impacts voluntourism can have. Simultaneously, while at UNC, I embarked on my first research endeavor by working part-time in the Department on Aging, Disability, and Long-Term Care at The UNC Cecil G. Sheps Center for Health Services Research. During my last semester at UNC, I continued to explore the world of research by working as a contractor at RTI International as a Research Assistant for the RTI-UNC Child Health Project and Smoking Study where I interviewed middle school children and their parents about their health behaviors.

After graduating from UNC, my first full-time job was working at the Duke Global Health Institute as a Research Assistant at the Duke Global Digital Health Science Center (formerly Duke

Obesity Prevention Program). In this role, I created study materials and protocols and conducted surveys and physical assessments with study participants. A year later, in 2014, I joined the U.S. Peace Corps as a Community Health Volunteer in the Southern Province (Gisagara District) of Rwanda. For two years, I became immersed in Public Health through community-based programming, health education, and career development. Although I was introduced to quantitative and qualitative data collection work while at UNC, through my Peace Corps experience, I was able to conduct a community needs assessment for the first time and contribute to the development of community-engaged programs and activities. My Peace Corps experience solidified my interest in program implementation beyond and with the goal of using data effectively and collaboratively to improve public health outcomes.

In August 2016, one month after my return to the U.S., I began a Master of Public Health (MPH) program at Emory University Rollins School of Public Health, with a concentration in Global Epidemiology. During my time at Emory, I was able to revisit my experience in Rwanda through HIV and family planning research with the Rwanda Zambia HIV Research Group. In this position, I co-designed data collection tools - specifically, surveys and focus group discussion guides. One of the most enjoyable parts of this experience for me was working with Community Health Workers to conduct these surveys and focus group discussions in local health clinics in the capital, Kigali. This work influenced my continued role as a research assistant at Emory for my second year, in which I completed the qualitative analysis and manuscript writing for this scope of work, and served as the Monitoring and Evaluation (M&E) point of contact for the family planning uptake program designed from this research. This research was also the basis of my thesis (and first publication), in which I analyzed the quantitative data through exploring factors associated with interest in postpartum intrauterine device (IUD) uptake among pregnant women and couples in Kigali, Rwanda.

After graduation, it was time to pack my bags once again. I moved to Pretoria, South Africa in September 2018, where I worked as an Epidemiology Fellow at the Centers for Disease Control and Prevention (CDC) in South Africa. This role was part of the PHI/CDC Global Health Fellowship Program, which is no longer an active fellowship program. In this role, I served as CDC South Africa's Data Manager and Analyst to support South Africa's quality site improvement program aimed at improving HIV case finding, treatment, and retention in HIV care in the President's Emergency Plan for AIDS Relief (PEPFAR)-funded health facilities.

When the COVID-19 pandemic reached the states in March 2020, I was evacuated from South Africa since fellows were required to evacuate. I did not return to South Africa upon accepting a new position as a Data Analysis Advisor (contractor) at the U.S. Agency for International Development (USAID). I worked in USAID's Global Health Bureau, Office of HIV/AIDS from October 2020-August 2023. This role was where I further leaned into my strength and interest in data strategy, advising, training, analysis, and visualization, which influenced my desire to launch and grow my business, Chilombo Consulting, into what it is today. Although the majority of my work was virtual, one international work trip took me to Rwanda, yet again, where I was able to support the HIV team's technical advisors and M&E staff with their analytical needs. My time back in Rwanda reminded me of what originally sparked my interest in global health work - the opportunity to connect with others in which I share both differences and similarities in cultural background and a vision of improving public health outcomes.

It was during my time at USAID that I applied my passion for career development to Diversity, Equity, Inclusion,

Accessibility and Workforce Development. For much of my time at USAID, I led the Human Resources (HR) Management & Hiring Committee for the Office of HIV/AIDS Anti-Racism/ Diversity, Equity, Inclusion, and Accessibility (DEIA) Working Group. In this role, I worked with the committee to conduct research on, advocate for, and implement equitable strategies in hiring, promotion, and retention. I was back to turning research data into action - what originally spearheaded my passion into a data-focused public health career after my Peace Corps service.

Stepping Into My Calling

Before my business, Chilombo Consulting, was born, my entrepreneurial efforts were originally focused on career consulting. After years of helping students, friends, and family members improve their resumes, practice interviewing, land scholarships, and secure jobs, my older sister suggested that I start a business and charge for my services. I resisted at first, but the saying that big sisters know best is actually true! On January 21, 2019, I incorporated my first business, and in March of 2021, I added Chilombo Consulting as a DBA (Doing Business As) to the original business name. We received our first consulting contract in July of that year. I was motivated to incorporate data consulting into the business when I started receiving one-off requests for analytical support. I also had the desire to contribute to Public Health and other sectors that were outside of the scope of my full-time role. I wanted to engage in public health work in an interdisciplinary way and consulting allowed me to do just that. Although my original intention with entrepreneurship was never to have it be my full-time role, I loved the diversity of the work, freedom of project selection, and opportunity to collaborate with employees, consultants, and business owners across different organizations and sectors. In June 2023, I closed down the career services operations to focus solely on data consulting.

On August 15, 2023, four and a half years after starting my entrepreneurial journey, I stepped down from my position at USAID and transitioned to full-time consulting! It was a challenging decision as I had a wonderful supervisor and team. However, I knew that I could no longer balance a full-time role with a growing business, especially as we had just landed our first year-long contract. I credit this book's visionary author, Quisha, for her resources which contributed to me making this decision with a strategy and positive mindset. Her session on creating an exit strategy really resonated with me, and after drafting one, reviewing my goals, progress, and risk level, I knew I couldn't wait another year for the 'perfect time' to take the leap of faith.

Chilombo Consulting offers services that help organizations make sense of their quantitative and qualitative data through four main areas:
- **Data Design and Strategy**
- **Data Collection, Analytics and Visualization**
- **Monitoring and Evaluation**
- **Data Coaching and Training**

We have consulted with universities, non-profit organizations, clinics, and other consulting firms as subcontractors to execute projects in the areas of public health, workforce development, DEIA, and education. We have advised, coached, and trained others on data processes or skills, and produced reporting guidance, standard operating procedures (SOPs), data collection tools, data analysis plans, cleaned datasets, descriptive and statistical analyses, dashboard mockups, interactive dashboards, reports, infographics, lesson plans, and presentations.

To ensure the success of my business as a Public Health Consultant, I focus on four key areas on a day-to-day:
1. **Business management and operations**: This includes ensuring Chilombo is compliant on all

accounts; updated on all contracts, invoices, and payments (for both contractors and clients); adequately staffed for projects; and that we are on budget and on task with our priorities and strategic goals.

2. **Business outreach and communications:** This includes following up with potential leads via emails and scheduled calls, sending inquiries to new leads, engaging in virtual business groups to contribute resources, set-up meet and greets, and respond to collaboration/proposal opportunities.

3. **Proposal development:** This includes reviewing applications, referral inquiries, and formal requests for proposals (RFPs); drafting responses (narratives, budget); and compiling references and work samples.

4. **Client work & project management:** This consists of meeting with the internal team for updates or strategy meetings, meeting with the client, and the hands-on work. Managing projects through tracking timelines, communicating progress and next steps is also a major component of my day-to-day responsibilities as a Public Health Consultant.

It's also important to note that I have 1099 contractors for support across all areas. As of 2024, I hired an Operations Assistant that assists with the first two categories and consultants who contribute to the last two categories. Additionally, I also spend time, although not daily, on **Business and Professional Development.**

Challenges Faced

A common challenge faced by Public Health Consultants is the expectation versus reality of project timelines and how it may conflict with doing equitable work. From my experience, responding to inquiries from referrals and from Request for Proposals (RFPs), I've found that the timelines may not align with the reality of doing the work with the full considerations and communications that would allow for a more equitable and inclusive process. There is often a sense of urgency to complete a project in a three-month time period that could benefit from a longer time period to thoroughly build rapport and engagement. This also includes the fact that Public Health Consultants often have more than one project ongoing at any given time. This may create a bias towards larger scale consulting firms that have human resources to move with this sense of urgency, which ultimately may take away from the requests to give preference to consultants who work independently or with a smaller boutique firm. Within this challenge, it's important to acknowledge the limited funding in many public health projects, which creates this additional barrier. Additionally, we must also acknowledge that in some cases, the work may be urgent. I advocate for a more transparent RFP process and recommend that organizations looking to hire Public Health Consultants also seek expert support from an equity advisor on the development of their RFPs.

Keeping Up with Industry Trends
Like in any business, it's important to keep up with the trends in my industry to ensure I'm remaining relevant for my clients. LinkedIn is my go-to social network for public health trends and trends that have public health implications. As I am connected with public health professionals across many different disciplines, individuals tend to share articles and events related to their specialty. Specifically, in the area of career development, I collaborate with a friend and fellow consultant to share trends and opportunities related to public health jobs and hiring opportunities on our LinkedIn page, *Public Health Resources*.

Additional certifications and training programs may also be useful. Before starting a certification or training program, however, I recommend that you reflect on your current or desired consulting services and hone in on programs that allow you to refine the skills needed to be successful in your niche. There are so many certifications and training programs out there, but not all may be needed or helpful to your desired consulting scope. Focus on professional development opportunities that incorporate projects and real-world activities, beyond just the consumption of information. For example, I recently completed the 'Masterclass on Facilitation Skills for Monitoring and Evaluation Professionals' by Ann-Murray Brown. I recommend this course for any public health consultant who is looking to refine how they navigate a group through a decision-making process, regardless of if they're the formal facilitator or subject matter expert in the room. As a data consultant, my work isn't just sitting behind my computer crunching numbers. A huge portion of my time is spent facilitating discussions with clients to make decisions regarding different elements of their data processes - whether it's the survey design, metric selection for monitoring and evaluation, or dashboard development. This course provided me with tangible practices, resources, and engaging tools that I've incorporated into my client work involving group interactions.

I foresee even more opportunities for public health consulting to expand beyond traditional public health and healthcare organizations. Even if aspiring and current public health consultants aim to focus on serving primarily public health organizations, it will be important to stay informed about public health in other industries and contexts. For those who wish to expand their skill sets outside of the traditional public health environment, keeping up with the literature and thought leaders while also completing any relevant training and attending informational webinars will be key to staying prepared and informed so that you can adapt your skill set as needed. For example, as workforce development and the future of work has become a focus of research and engagement across the U.S., as it is an interest of mine, I have been able to keep up with the subject area through literature, thought leadership, and advocacy in my online community. Additionally, the work experiences and lived experiences of my consultants and myself contribute to our ability to consult on projects within this scope.

Relationship Building
Building relationships with clients and stakeholders requires a great deal of intentionality. Taking the time to understand the organization and its intended outcomes is key for building rapport. For truly effective impact through your engagement, your work should be collaborative, and through understanding the context, you and your client are more likely to set realistic expectations from the beginning. This essentially allows the organization and consulting team to better adapt to changes while staying on task throughout the project period.

Another way is through keeping open channels of communication and a space for your client to provide insights and feedback, to ultimately improve the process and outcome of the project. Just because consultants are experts in their services, doesn't mean there won't be room for improvement and pivoting. Ensuring that there's a space for different types of communication will allow you to deliver quality, informed, and tailored solutions. For example, my team and I are currently working on a one-year contract with a client (which includes a non-profit and its funded partners). For this consultancy, we advised them on metric development, documented reporting guidance for the data collection process, and set up a streamlined data cleaning, analysis, and dashboard development process. A major part of this work is facilitating discussions to come to a consensus on the metrics and analytical questions of interest to monitor in the dashboard. During these discussions and in our follow-up email communications, we work to ensure that everyone is able to provide input. Moreover, from the recommendation of one of my team members, we conducted a pulse check (with the option to be semi-anonymous) at the end of the first phase of the project, so we could move forward in the new year with additional considerations and best practices. One of the recommendations we received during the pulse check allowed us to facilitate a discussion where the partners came to a consensus on partner accountability regarding pre-work and meeting attendance.

Diversity and Inclusion

In the world of data, one of the biggest barriers to developing effective public health strategies for diverse communities is the lack of relevant data as well as, specifically, qualitative, contextual data to tell the full story. As a data consultant, this often starts with data collection. Making sure that we can capture different experiences through tailored surveys, interviews, and focus groups is key. Not only having the data, but also analyzing it so that we can understand differences within the population, is also important. Chilombo Consulting's values include working with equity-focused organizations that have taken into account the needs and desires of those participating in the program and not relying only on the views of the organization with power or oversight. This allows us to continue our work to develop actionable insights based on data that is inclusive and comprehensive to the best of its ability, even when there are barriers such as funding or time constraints to a comprehensive data collection process. Ensuring that we communicate these findings with different experiences highlighted is an important strategy. For example, stratifying data by demographic and SDoH groups where appropriate can provide tailored and human-centered recommendations that lend to effective public health strategies for diverse communities.

Making An Impact

As a data consulting firm, improving public health outcomes are demonstrated through our ability to design tools, analyze data, and communicate insights that can effectively measure public health outcomes. In 2022, I worked on a project in which I supported a nonprofit organization in adapting a tool focused on measuring the quality of care in the Sexual and Reproductive Health (SRH) sector. I developed an Excel-based tool that calculated scores used to assess specific outcomes based on the data entered in by the users who support clinics with their SRH programming. My contribution to this project allowed them to translate a less accessible statistical software tool to a universal and more accessible and adaptable Excel-based tool, so that healthcare providers in all socioeconomic contexts could not only monitor these SRH metrics that were relevant to their context, but use them to take actions where needed for improvements and ongoing maintenance. Although I am not engaged in the project on an ongoing basis to monitor the usage of this tool (another challenge when it comes to short-term consulting!), as it is accessible on their website as a global resource and routinely publicized through their communication channels, I am confident that it is making an impact on public health outcomes.

My greatest success and lesson learned in consulting was in my pivot from career to data consulting. From February 2023 to May 2023, I participated in the One Million Black Women: Black in Business Program by Goldman Sachs. This program was my first structured program in which I was formally trained on concrete business skills such as building customer profiles, incorporating systems for growth, marketing, and financial management. I was originally accepted into this program for my career consulting business, so I went through the 10-week program focused on the growth and refinement of that business. At the end of the program, and after having my best performing month of the career consulting business to date, I found that it was actually the data consulting business that I wanted to grow into a full-scale business. Career development is a passion of mine and will always be something I do, but this program gave me the clarity I needed to restructure my business. In June 2023, I permanently closed down the career consulting services. I encourage you to explore business programs that align with your journey and knowledge gaps, but most importantly, that inspire you to embrace the pivot!

Work-Life Balance
It's so easy to become immersed in business. It's what we love. It's who we are. Recognizing that work-life balance is important, however, is what will ultimately lead to a more fulfilling, sustainable career. I've incorporated the following to ensure I maintain balance between the two:

> **Calendar blocking:** I balance out my work schedule by scheduling breaks into my day. I also have dedicated days for availability in my schedule for meet and greets and project discovery calls.
>
> **Meeting-free Fridays:** I rarely take meetings on Fridays. Fridays are my day for priorities outside of Chilombo Consulting and to get a headstart on the weekend.
>
> **Boundary-setting & planning:** Where feasible, I plan a recurring meeting schedule for internal team and external client meetings. Even though flexibility in consulting is vital, setting boundaries and communicating them, such as your meeting availability and capacity is just as important to avoid burnout.

Beyond the Book - People Skills
Active listening and proactiveness are two skills beyond the technical expertise that I've found to be instrumental in my journey as a public health consultant.

Active Listening: Although you are being hired for your specific expertise - whether it's for strategic planning, data analysis, curriculum development, or program planning, your ability to do so is only effective and collaborative when you truly listen, process, and ask questions before contributing to the work. Active listening should occur throughout a project and not just during proposal or project kick-off meetings.

Proactiveness: Public Health Consultants must be proactive, both in their business operations and client work. From the business standpoint, there is proactiveness in seeking out and vetting services you may need (i.e. lawyers, accountants, website developers) as well as in processes you need to maintain (i.e. business registrations, certifications, insurance). You must also be proactive in how you connect with others and market your services. I do this through my Business and Professional Development scope of work which includes attending business training and networking events in my state, writing thought leadership posts on LinkedIn, and joining different business communities virtually (i.e Quisha's group - PublicHealthPreneurs: Make Impact & Income) and in-person (i.e. Black Chamber of Commerce).

Encouragement for Aspiring Public Health Consultants
If your goal is to pursue public health entrepreneurship, my advice is to do your internal and external research so you can understand what services you can offer that align with both your skill set and the demand. Develop an exit strategy from your current job (including an updated personal and business budget and financial plan). Map out your business in terms of your mission, vision, values, ideal clients,

services, and SMART Goals. This is the foundation of a business or strategic plan, which you can continue to iterate on as you build your business. Start compiling contacts that know the quality of your work. When I started with career consulting, my first testimonials were from the individuals I had helped for free for the three years prior. In the context of consulting with organizations, even if you can't yet promote your services to an organizational contact due to a potential conflict of interest, still add them to your internal list. As I am still early in my consulting career, I still often reference my previous work experiences alongside my consulting experiences when pitching or responding to project opportunities. Keep in mind that there is no traditional path or perfect time to transition into public health consulting and entrepreneurship, and if you're currently employed full or part-time, start your business while you still have that position. In short, take action now!

I started my public health career consulting business at the age of 27 (eight months after obtaining my MPH) and public health data consulting at 29. To some this may seem too young or early in a career, but I was confident in my data, project management, and communication skill sets to take consulting head-on. My journey is still fresh, but through working on my mindset, continuing to build my skills, and having an exit strategy, financial plan, and alternative pivot plans in place, I was able to leave a six-figure government contractor position to pursue public health consulting and entrepreneurship full-time. It's also important to acknowledge that everyone's circumstances are different which influences their risk level and specific considerations for transitioning into full-time entrepreneurship. For example, I currently have private and federal student loan debt; however, I was able to start my journey in full-time entrepreneurship with six months of expenses saved.

Ideal Client

My ideal clients are organizations (consulting firms, nonprofits, universities, and government contractors) that are looking to operationalize their data processes and make sense of their quantitative and qualitative data. They are equity-centered organizations, meaning that they don't work in silos among just their staff, but they are actively working towards an inclusive approach, to ensure that diverse recommendations are heard and incorporated into the project, program, or organization's culture. Additionally, they are organizations that are not only focused on centering equity with the populations they serve, but also within their own staff and workforce.

I love working on projects where we get to utilize mixed methods - both quantitative and qualitative data. Although my start in public health was in quantitative data from an epidemiology focus, I simultaneously trained in qualitative methods throughout my time in graduate school. One of my favorite experiences while in graduate school was serving as a Teaching Assistant for the Qualitative Methods course. When I started Chilombo Consulting, the focus was solely on quantitative focused projects, but as we grew and I encountered more opportunities, I often thought to myself "this would benefit from qualitative methods." When I received my first project inquiry to work on a mixed methods analysis and presentation development project, I knew I had found the missing piece to the puzzle of Chilombo Consulting's unique value proposition. The mixed methods approach enriches discussions and allows for more nuanced recommendations to ultimately provide clients with the most comprehensive insights for action.

Potential clients can connect with me by visiting my website: https://chilomboconsulting.com, messaging me on LinkedIn: www.linkedin.com/in/vcdacosta, or emailing: hello@chilomboconsulting.com.

Acknowledgements: I would like to acknowledge my parents, sisters, friends, and partner for their unwavering support during my transition into full-time entrepreneurship. Chinonye, thanks for being my first entrepreneur friend, advisor, and motivator! I would also like to thank our visionary author, Quisha, for her resources and community that played a major role in my decision to take this leap. I'd like to thank all my contractors for their contributions and expertise, and specifically a shout out to Brittney and Asya for their leadership across both client work and business development. Additionally, I'd like to thank my former supervisor at USAID, Ramona, for her genuine interest in and commitment to my professional growth within and beyond my role.

"No one becomes an entrepreneur to live paycheck to paycheck." – Quisha Umemba

Part 3 - Profit: The Path to a Profitable (and Sustainable) Public Health Consulting Business

Introduction
Chances are you picked up this book because you are curious about public health entrepreneurship. Maybe you are a helping professional eager to amplify your impact and you were drawn in by the title. Maybe you've already embarked on your entrepreneurial journey but aren't seeing the impact or income you hoped for. Perhaps you're reading for a dose of inspiration from the success stories my colleagues and I shared. If any of these resonate with you and you're wondering how to leverage years of education and expertise to start, grow, and scale a thriving public health consulting business, keep reading! Whether you're at the beginning of your journey or aiming to broaden your impact, the upcoming chapters will introduce you to my step-by-step system designed to help you turn your passion for public health into a profitable endeavor, one step at a time.

In Chapter 8, "**Starting Your Public Health Business**," I examine the critical aspects of perspective and mindset mastery, recognizing the importance of cultivating the right mindset to thrive as an entrepreneur. I also explore the significance of positioning your business in the marketplace and marketing your expertise.

In Chapter 9, "**Growing Your Public Health Business**," we shift our focus to the pivotal stages of business expansion where I will discuss pricing strategies to help you monetize your skillset. In this chapter, I provide invaluable insights into setting rates and maximizing your earning potential. I also explore the art of packaging and branding when it comes to crafting a compelling brand narrative and differentiating yourself in the competitive landscape of public health consulting.

Profit: The Path to a Profitable (and Sustainable) Public Health Consulting Business

Finally, in Chapter 10, **"Scaling Your Public Health Business,"** I turn your attention to systems and processes that will propel your business to new heights. First, I discuss the importance of optimizing your processes, streamlining your operations, enhancing efficiency to drive sustainable growth, and finally, the art of pitching, equipping you with the skills and strategies to attract and retain clients and scale your business ventures with confidence.

As you read the chapters that follow, you'll learn to bridge the gap between purpose and profit, and how to address pressing public health issues while also building a profitable and sustainable business venture. Together, these chapters will serve as your roadmap to entrepreneurial success, guiding you through the essential steps of starting, growing, and scaling a thriving public health business venture.

Chapter 8:
Starting Your Public Health Business

Introduction
In my journey, I've encountered an array of public health entrepreneurs from diverse backgrounds, and they are all bound by a shared commitment to advance public health through entrepreneurial innovation. I've seen this passion transcend from theory to practice, with individuals who have pioneered initiatives that are not only ethically motivated but also economically viable. Their stories, like the ones shared in this book, represent a shift where passion and purpose drive the creation of those initiatives. By infusing entrepreneurial thinking into public health, we enhance the effectiveness of health interventions while also promoting sustainable solutions. Entrepreneurs in the public health space are overlooked in public health discourse but our work at the intersection of business and societal good is nothing short of revolutionary, offering a unique opportunity to address the complex challenges facing our world today. The ever-evolving landscape of health issues demands innovative and adaptive solutions, and it all starts with embracing the entrepreneurial mindset.

Embracing the Entrepreneurial Mindset
Every exceptional business coach knows that cultivating an entrepreneurial mindset is the first step of the coaching process. The importance of your mindset cannot be overstated—it is critical to your success as an entrepreneur. In fact, many coaches insist on a well-developed mindset before they agree to work with you. A colleague and fellow nurse consultant, Quinta Caylor, goes as far as offering the mindset module of her coaching program for free because she "can't work with coaching clients until their mind is on good soil." This approach underscores the foundational role a positive and resilient mindset plays in paving the way for success in the entrepreneurial journey. What I will share with you in this

chapter is no different. When it comes to entrepreneurship, success is not solely determined by the product or service offered, but rather by the mindset and positioning of the entrepreneur behind it. The journey of building a public health business is as much about mastering one's mindset as it is about developing expertise in the field.

Mindset, often described as the lens through which we view the world and approach challenges, serves as the foundation upon which all entrepreneurial endeavors are built. Adopting an entrepreneurial mindset entails embracing qualities such as resilience, adaptability, and a willingness to take calculated risks. As public health entrepreneurs navigate the complexities of starting, growing, and scaling their businesses, their mindset becomes a guiding force, influencing their decision-making processes and shaping their responses to adversity. The first step in the entrepreneurial journey is mindset mastery.

Perspective (Mastering Your Mindset)
Mindset is all about perspective – how you perceive yourself, the people surrounding you, and the world around you. Your mindset influences how you think, feel, and behave in any given situation. Being truly successful requires you to master your mindset. Why? You must have the drive, willingness, and belief that you can achieve bigger, better things in life to achieve bigger, better things in life! Mahatma Gandhi said, *"Your beliefs become your thoughts, your thoughts become your words, your words become your actions, your actions become your habits, your habits become your values, and your values become your destiny."* When you understand how each of these constructs influences another, it's easy to understand how the power of your thoughts ultimately shapes your future. Mastering your mindset is a crucial step for those considering entrepreneurship but you don't master your mindset overnight, it's a continual process. Mindset mastery plays a critical role in helping you achieve your goals because of its effect on how you see things, what you believe, and what you do. A lifetime of thinking and programming takes an entire paradigm shift to evolve into a new way of thinking and

behaving, but that's the work that needs to be done before and during your entrepreneurial journey.

More Than a Positive Outlook on Life

I'll be upfront with you—I didn't grasp the full significance of mindset or why it mattered so much until I embarked on my entrepreneurial journey. It wasn't until an experience with my second business coach that the concept of mindset clicked for me. Initially, I felt overwhelmed by the tasks she set before me, not realizing she was nudging me out of my comfort zone on purpose. "Quisha, you need to work on your mindset," she would constantly say to me, whether in our one-on-one meetings or in group sessions. At that time, I equated having a good mindset with maintaining a positive outlook. Yes, I considered myself a realist, but I've always leaned towards a positive perspective, choosing to see the glass as half full rather than half empty. So, I kept wondering, why does she insist I need to work on my mindset? But over time, I began to understand. Facing the challenges of a new entrepreneur—building my business, developing my brand, creating my products and services, and putting myself out there made me understand the importance of mindset. It is more than just being positive; it's about cultivating resilience, adaptability, confidence, and a readiness to embrace challenges head-on.

After this epiphany, I dove headfirst into books on entrepreneurship and the mindset that drives successful entrepreneurs. I was consumed with listening to business podcasts, immersing myself in the voices of those willingly sharing their lessons learned. I made a conscious decision to shift my inner circle, alter my thoughts, and be selective about what I allowed to influence me. Every day became a dedicated routine of reading and writing, and of committing to affirmations that I would recite in front of the mirror, affirming my worth and capabilities directly to my reflection. *"I am the answer to someone's problems. There are individuals, communities, organizations, and corporations who need my solutions, and my services are exactly what they have been looking for. I commit to expanding my impact, increasing my income, and securing my financial legacy."*

As I committed to my journey of mindset transformation, the changes began to manifest in both my personal and professional life. It was a powerful realization to see that the state of my mindset had a direct correlation with my outcomes. I understood that if I desired different results, a new mindset was not just beneficial—it was essential. This connection between mindset and results became a guiding principle for me, illuminating the path to growth and success.

Why Mindset Matters
I mentioned a powerful quote from Mahatma Gandhi earlier: *"Your beliefs become your thoughts, your thoughts become your words, your words become your actions, your actions become your habits, your habits become your values, and your values become your destiny."* Understanding the chain reaction from beliefs to destiny highlights the incredible influence our thoughts have on our future.

Now, allow me to tailor this concept specifically for you, the entrepreneur. *"Your mindset correlates with your attitude. Your attitude correlates with your behavior. Your behavior has a direct correlation with your actions or if you're working with clients, the solutions that you provide to your clients, which has a direct correlation to the results that you see as a business owner, which directly impacts performance individually and professionally."* This is precisely why nurturing a positive and resilient mindset is crucial. It's not just about thinking positively; it's about setting the foundation for success in every aspect of your entrepreneurial journey.

Building a Business Mindset and the Different Types of Mindsets
Adopting a CEO mindset means cultivating a business-oriented way of thinking. This mindset is essentially an approach or perspective that guides you toward making decisions that are both practical and strategic for your business. It's important to recognize that there are various mindsets out there, and some may come more naturally to you than others but with hard work and determination, anyone can

develop a CEO mindset. Below are some of the different types of mindsets you might encounter in business.

<u>Entrepreneur Mindset vs CEO Mindset</u>
The first step to becoming an entrepreneur is unlearning everything you were taught by people who aren't entrepreneurs. What does this mean? This means that being an entrepreneur requires a different mindset compared to traditional career paths. This is because entrepreneurship is all about taking risks, facing challenges, and coming up with innovative solutions. Entrepreneurship requires you to be adaptable and open-minded and successful entrepreneurship often requires breaking the rules, taking unconventional paths, and challenging norms. It means letting go of any limiting beliefs or doubts that may hold you back from pursuing your dreams. One of the things I struggled with most (as most people do) in the transition from being an employee to running my own business was slipping into the old "employee mindset".

An Employee Mindset often involves:
- A preoccupation with staying busy, with a primary focus on ticking off tasks from the immediate to-do list.

- Avoiding deep thought or strategic planning because these are seen as distractions from day-to-day activities.

- Hesitating to take bold steps until feeling "qualified" enough or until receiving approval from others, adhering to the belief that one must "pay their dues" and "put in their time" to gain opportunities.

- Equating personal value with the amount of time dedicated to work.

On the other hand, embracing a CEO mindset is about:

- Prioritizing outcomes such as revenue growth, profitability, customer retention, and efficient use of time, especially in activities that drive tangible results.
- Recognizing that time and, even more crucially, energy are your most significant resources, which should be invested wisely.
- Most importantly, having a clear vision for the future of your business, which guides all decision-making and aligns with long-term objectives.

Don't get me wrong, having an employee mindset can be extremely useful when it comes to delivering results in a particular area of your business, especially under time pressure or budget constraints. However, too many entrepreneurs are letting themselves be run by their to-do lists in an endless hamster wheel of busyness. And busyness is bad for business. If you run your business exclusively with an employee mindset, you'll quickly become overwhelmed and burned out, which is the opposite of what we want to achieve as entrepreneurs.

You can begin to embrace your CEO mindset with a deep dive into self-awareness. To enhance self-awareness, the key isn't to drown in the "whys" – "Why do I act this way? Why was my performance review disappointing? Why am I not making money?" Instead, shift your focus to the "whats" – "What situations trigger negative feelings in me? What steps can I take to perform better? What can I do to improve our marketing strategies?" By pivoting from why to what, you're more likely to uncover actionable insights and foster a deeper understanding of yourself as a CEO, a fundamental step in adopting a CEO mindset.

<u>Growth Mindset vs Fixed Mindset</u>
Embracing a growth mindset means believing in your ability to learn and expand your capabilities. It's about understanding that intelligence, talent, and skills can grow through dedication

and hard work. With a growth mindset, setbacks become stepping stones, offering valuable lessons and opportunities to adapt and improve. Conversely, a fixed mindset is rooted in the belief that intelligence and abilities are set in stone. This perspective can lead to a fear of failure, reluctance to embrace change, and the view that talent is limited. Such a mindset often results in stagnation and a continuous cycle of underachievement.

For those of us striving for more (what I like to refer to as "multi-passionate overachievers")—whether in education, business, or personal growth—a growth mindset propels us forward. It encourages us to face challenges head-on, persist through difficulties, and welcome constructive feedback as a chance to evolve. On the other hand, a fixed mindset traps us in a cycle of avoidance and defensiveness, hindering progress and opportunities for improvement. I've experienced firsthand the discomfort of receiving negative feedback, whether from a loved one or in a professional setting. It's not easy to hear. Yet, it's through developing resilience and a commitment to growth that I've learned to see such moments as chances to improve. This mindset shift has been transformative, not just in how I approach business, but in every aspect of my life.

If you're aiming to elevate your career, start a business, or simply become a more confident version of yourself, a fixed mindset won't get you far. I've seen individuals with this mindset give up before even starting because of the defeatist attitude that squanders their potential and opportunity. However, adopting a growth mindset transforms challenges into opportunities. Think of it as embodying the spirit of "the little engine that could," telling yourself, "I think I can" in the face of adversity. This mindset acknowledges that while obstacles are inevitable, they are also invaluable learning experiences. A growth mindset doesn't see failure as a reflection of your worth but as a chance to try anew. Cultivating a growth mindset over a fixed one is crucial for entrepreneurial success and the best way to start doing this is to start viewing every challenge as an opportunity for growth and every failure as a lesson leading to success.

Abundance Mindset vs Scarcity Mindset

Abundance and scarcity are two mindsets that shape our lives, our successes, and how we view the world around us. My father, a dedicated teacher and coach for more than 30 years, introduced these two concepts to my sisters and me when we were little girls and they have profoundly influenced my approach to life and business. Abundance is about feeling rich with what you have, and believing you're equipped with everything needed for fulfillment, happiness, and empowerment. It's knowing you are enough and will have enough. This mindset fills you with excitement, positivity, and hope, lighting up your path and lifting your ideas and feelings. In contrast, a scarcity mindset is feeling perpetually short of something, believing happiness and fulfillment are always just out of reach, and needing "more" to feel complete. It's a mindset clouded by fear and anxiety, limiting your ability to dream and see the vast array of possibilities that life offers. Scarcity keeps you playing it safe and small, hindering growth and positive transformation.

Stephen Covey, in *The 7 Habits of Highly Effective People*, describes scarcity as a win-lose scenario—believing that someone else's gain is your loss. However, he champions the abundance mindset as a win-win scenario, where there's enough for everyone, it fosters a sense of community and mutual success. Early in my entrepreneurial journey, I struggled with a scarcity mindset, hesitant to share my knowledge freely, fearing it would be stolen by others. This mindset held me back, keeping my expertise hidden and stifling my business growth. It was only when I embraced abundance, understanding that sharing what I knew could expand my reach and impact, that my public health consulting business began to thrive. I learned that generosity breeds abundance, and by contributing to the greater public health community, I was not only helping others but also enhancing my growth and opportunities.

To shift towards abundance, start by assessing what you have to offer. Transform negative thoughts into positive affirmations, practice gratitude, and embrace collaboration, knowing that giving and receiving are part of the same cycle. Developing discernment to balance giving and receiving is critical in entrepreneurship, but the core lies in believing in the abundance of opportunities, resources, and possibilities available to us all. This mindset shift is not just about personal gain but about contributing to a larger ecosystem where everyone can thrive. It's about moving from a place of competition to one of contribution and collaboration, recognizing that there is, indeed, enough "pie" for everyone to eat.

Practical Advice to Help Shift Your Perspective
Stay Learning
- Stay informed about the latest trends and developments in public health and business.
- Read books, attend workshops, and participate in webinars related to entrepreneurship and your area of expertise.
- Learn from other successful entrepreneurs. This could be through mentorship, networking, or studying their career paths and strategies.

Develop a Problem-Solving Attitude
- Approach challenges as opportunities to learn and grow.
- Be adaptable and willing to pivot strategies when necessary.
- Practice critical thinking and always look for innovative solutions to problems.

Build Resilience
- Understand that failure is a part of the entrepreneurial journey. Learn from setbacks rather than being discouraged by them.

- Maintain a positive attitude and stay focused on your vision, even when faced with challenges.
- Practice self-care and stress management to maintain your health and well-being.

Practice Decision-Making
- Get comfortable making decisions with the information you have, knowing that not all decisions will be perfect.
- Learn to trust your instincts while also relying on data and research to guide your choices.
- Reflect on the outcomes of your decisions to improve your decision-making skills over time.

Foster Innovation and Creativity
- Encourage yourself to think outside the box and explore new ideas. Challenge the status quo.
- Stay open to new technologies and methodologies that could enhance your business.
- Create a culture of innovation within your business, where new ideas are welcomed and explored.

Finally - adopt a purpose-driven, profit-focused mantra and lifestyle. Your new slogan must be "make impact and income". Understanding and cultivating the right mindset can lead to more effective behavior, better decision-making, and increased success in various aspects of life, especially in business. Remember, this is a journey of personal and professional growth. Each step you take builds your confidence and capabilities as an entrepreneur in the public health sector.

Positioning (Marketing Your Expertise)
Positioning is about strategically "marking your territory" in your industry. It's how you define your business's desired

perception in the market and set it apart from the competition. Essentially, it's your way of "letting your light shine", establishing yourself as a thought leader, and showcasing your expertise to prospects, clients, and partners. Here's a simplified four-step process to get started:

1. Identify Your Market and Stake Your Claim

Determine your target market or industry and your specific audience within that market. You can do as I did and start by identifying your own background and interests. My background in nursing and public health naturally led me to serve clients within those same fields. While pinpointing my market was straightforward, defining my target audience required more effort. For example, my target market includes public health organizations and healthcare systems, whereas my target audience is public health professionals. This means that the entity that pays me for services isn't always the same audience that I'm serving. Does that make sense?

2. Build Your Authority and Develop a Platform

You might think you need to know everything about a subject to be an expert. Not true. An expert has "authoritative knowledge" on a topic. Some would argue that knowing just a bit more than your audience knows makes you an expert. Building your authority (credibility and thought leadership) is crucial to building a successful business. Without authority, it's difficult for people to know, like, and trust you. If you want people to buy what you are selling and "buy in" to your messaging, then you must build your authority to develop a platform. Here are some general ways to build your authority:

- *Specialize in a Niche:* By focusing on a specific niche or industry, you can establish yourself as an expert in that area. Remember you can't serve everybody, and you shouldn't. Pick one specialty and run with it. (What can you teach or talk about for sixty minutes without preparation? Chances are, that's your specialty.)

- *Create Quality Content:* Share your knowledge and expertise through blog posts, videos, podcasts, or any other form of content. This will not only showcase your expertise but also help you reach a larger audience.

- *Connect with Other Experts:* Collaborate with other experts in your field to gain more credibility and exposure.

- *Build a Strong Online Presence:* In today's digital age, having a strong online presence is essential for building your authority. Create and maintain professional profiles on social media platforms and engage with your audience regularly.

- *Gain Experience:* This is extremely important. The more experience you have in your field, the more authority you will have. Get involved in projects, volunteer work or internships to gain hands-on experience. (Note to public health students: Please get work experience before starting a public health consulting business. The experience is as much for you as it is for the clients you strive to serve. That's all I will say on that matter, for now.)

3. Define Your Unique Value Proposition (UVP):
Your UVP highlights what makes your consulting services unique. A UVP is a clear and concise statement that explains what you offer, how it solves your clients' problems, and why they should choose you over your competitors. Creating a UVP requires careful consideration and understanding of your target audience, their pain points, and how your services can address them. Here are some steps to help you define your unique value proposition:

- *Understand Your Target Audience* - The first step in creating a UVP is understanding your target audience. This includes their demographics, behavior, needs, and pain points. Conduct market research and engage with your potential clients to gather this information.

- *Identify Your Competitors* - Identify who your main competitors are and what they offer. This will help you understand your market positioning and what sets you apart from the rest.

- *Analyze Your Services* - Take a deep dive into your services and analyze what makes them unique. Consider the benefits they provide, any special features or expertise, and how they solve your clients' problems.

- *Focus on Benefits* - When creating your UVP, focus on the benefits your services provide rather than just listing their features. This will help potential clients understand how your consultancy can add value to their business.

- *Be Clear and Concise* - Your UVP should be easy to understand and communicate. Avoid using technical jargon or complicated language. Keep it short and to the point, no more than two sentences.

Here are my UVPs:
Umemba Health - "Umemba Health helps public health organizations and healthcare systems to educate their workforce, empower their leadership, and expand their community presence to elevate the lives of the individuals and communities they serve."

Quisha Umemba Consulting - "I teach helping professionals how to leverage their expertise, package their genius, and monetize their skillset to start, grow, and scale a profitable public health consulting business that makes impact and income."

Now it's your turn. Use the formula below to come up with your own unique UVP.

UVP Formula
Who are you? (How do you identify?)
Who do you serve? (Target audience/ideal client/niche)
How do you serve? (What pain point do you address?)
Why do you serve? (Optional)

4. Share Your Expertise with the World
Claiming your expertise isn't enough; you must share it with the world. Look for opportunities to showcase your expertise, such as speaking engagements, podcasts, guest blogging, presenting at conferences, or hosting webinars and workshops. Start by building a community of loyal supporters (or followers) with the goal being quality supporters, not quantity. Gaining loyalty and trust takes time, but it's crucial for building a supportive base. Understand that while some may quickly decide to work with you, most need to build trust first. Increasing your visibility is essential for doing this. Platforms like Facebook, Twitter, Instagram, and LinkedIn are invaluable for building social credibility. If social media isn't your forte, guess what, it wasn't for me initially either. I had to learn to get comfortable with being uncomfortable. Mindset mastery, as I'm sure you've probably guessed, is critical for this step. Be prepared to tackle fear, imposter syndrome, perfectionism, and self-doubt. All of these are barriers that can hold you back if not addressed.

Building Credibility and Thought Leadership
Establishing credibility and thought leadership is essential for public health entrepreneurs aiming to market their expertise effectively. The key to establishing thought leadership is consistency and authenticity. Regularly sharing valuable insights and engaging with your target market and audience can significantly enhance your credibility and position you as a go-to expert in your area. Below are several strategies that can help you achieve this:

Publishing Insightful Content
Write articles, blog posts, or white papers on current public health issues, trends, and innovations. This content can be published on your website, LinkedIn, industry journals, or public health blogs. Focus on topics where you have deep knowledge or unique perspectives. Something that helps you to stand out and sets you apart in your field.

Speaking Engagements
Seek opportunities to speak at conferences, webinars, workshops, and panel discussions related to areas of expertise in public health. These platforms allow you to share your knowledge and insights with a broader audience, enhancing your visibility and credibility.

Hosting Educational Webinars and Workshops
Organize and host webinars or workshops on specific public health topics. This not only showcases your expertise but also helps in building a community of professionals interested in your area of specialization.

Participating in Podcasts and Interviews
Either start your own podcast focusing on public health topics or be a guest on existing podcasts. Interviews, whether on podcasts, in videos, or print media, can also be a powerful way to share your story and expertise.

Social Media Engagement
Actively engage on social media platforms like LinkedIn, Twitter, and Instagram. Share your insights, comment on relevant posts, and participate in discussions. This consistent engagement helps in building a following and establishing your voice in the field.

Networking and Collaborations
Build relationships with other public health professionals, organizations, and influencers. Collaborating on projects, research, or community initiatives can enhance your reputation and expand your reach.

Offering Expert Commentary
Be available to provide expert commentary on public health issues to media outlets. This could involve commenting on current public health news, contributing to articles, or participating in television or radio interviews.

Publishing Case Studies and Success Stories
Share case studies or success stories from your work, highlighting how you've addressed public health challenges effectively. This not only demonstrates your expertise but also provides tangible proof of your impact.

Continuous Learning and Certification
Stay updated with the latest public health knowledge and skills. Attending courses, workshops, and obtaining certifications can add to your credibility.

Engaging in Community Service
Participate in or lead community health initiatives. Serve on a board of directors or an advisory committee. This not only contributes to societal well-being but also showcases leadership abilities as well as your commitment and expertise to the field in a particular setting.

By implementing these strategies, you'll not only position yourself effectively in your industry but also build a solid foundation for marketing your expertise and growing your public health consulting business.

Chapter 9:
Growing Your Public Health Consulting Business

Introduction
In Chapter 2, we delved into the current state of the public health consulting landscape, drawing on the insights from a study by Roman et al titled, "Describing the Self-Employed Public Health Consultant and Entrepreneur Workforce in the United States – A Survey Snapshot for Consultants." This research provided us with a glimpse into the average hourly rates for public health consultants, as reported by the 119 qualified survey respondents. However, we stopped short of exploring the specifics of how to monetize your expertise and determine the appropriate fees for your consulting services. In this chapter, we will dive deeper into the topic of monetizing your expertise as a public health consultant.

Pricing (Monetizing Your Skillset)
As a public health entrepreneur, it is important to understand how to monetize your expertise and set appropriate fees for your consulting services. This process involves considering various factors such as the level of experience, skills, and knowledge you possess in your specific area of expertise. Additionally, it requires conducting market research and evaluating industry standards for similar services. Your ultimate goal as a public health consultant is to make impact and income, so it's important for you to adopt a pricing model that considers your client's budget with the value you provide. Understanding the dynamics that influence pricing trends is crucial for consultants aiming to set competitive, yet fair, rates for their services. Here are key factors to consider:
- *Economic Climate and Global Events:* The overall economic environment and global happenings can

significantly impact pricing trends, affecting client budgets and project availability.

- *Geographic Location:* Where you or your clients are based can influence pricing, due to cost-of-living differences and local market rates. This is true even if you work remotely.

- *Consultant Expertise:* Your level of experience and depth of expertise allow you to charge more. The more seasoned and knowledgeable you are, the higher the rates you can command.

- *Project Complexity:* Projects that involve collaboration across multiple sectors, partners, and interventions often warrant higher fees. The complexity of these projects justifies a higher rate, as they require a deeper level of expertise and effort. For instance, while offering program design services may command one fee, providing a comprehensive package that includes design, implementation, and evaluation services would understandably justify a different, higher fee.

The Public Health Consultant's Pricing Playbook
The steps below have been designed as a starting point for you as you refine your pricing structure and gain more insight and experience over time. By systematically reflecting on these aspects, you can gain a clearer understanding of your professional identity and how to effectively position yourself in the market. This reflection not only aids in setting the direction for your consulting practice but also ensures that they remain aligned with your core values and areas of expertise. It's important that you periodically review and adjust your pricing structure to stay competitive and ensure it aligns with your evolving expertise and the market dynamics.

Step 1: Self-Assessment
On a separate piece of paper, reflect on your unique skills, experiences, and areas of expertise in public health.

- List all of your formal qualifications (For example: MPH, BSN, RN, CDCES, CHWI)
- List all of your technical skills (epi, biostatistics, program evaluation, etc.)
- List the soft skills that you possess (leadership, communication, cultural competency, etc).

Chronicle Your Career Path
- Reflect on your journey in public health. What roles have you held? What projects have you led or contributed to? This could range from clinical work as a nurse to designing public health programs or policies.
- Assess your impact and achievements: Think about the outcomes of your work. What changes or improvements have you facilitated? How have your efforts impacted communities or organizations?

Areas of Specialization
- Identify Your Niche: Do you specialize in a particular area of public health, like infectious diseases, community health, health education, or chronic disease management?
- Consider Your Passion: What areas in public health are you most passionate about? This passion often translates into more enthusiasm and expertise in your work.

Develop Your Unique Value Proposition/Unique Selling Proposition
- Define What Sets You Apart: Consider what makes your consulting service unique. Is it your blended expertise in nursing and public health? Your approach to training and workforce development? Your ability to translate complex health information into actionable strategies?

- Articulate Your UVP: Craft a statement that encapsulates your unique blend of skills, experiences, and passion. This will be a key element in marketing your consulting services. Refer to the UVP formula in Chapter 8.

Step 2: Identify Your Service Offerings
Identify Gaps in the Market
- Research current trends and needs in the public health sector. Are there emerging issues or underserved areas where your expertise could be particularly valuable?
- Look at what other public health consultants are offering. Identify services that are in high demand but have less competition.

Align with Target Audience Needs
- Define your target audience. Are they government agencies, non-profits, healthcare facilities, or community organizations?
- Understand the specific challenges and needs of your target audience. How can your expertise address these challenges?

Develop Signature Services
- Based on your expertise and market needs, create a list of potential services you can offer. These could range from program development and evaluation to training workshops or policy analysis.
- Consider how you can package these services in a way that is both appealing and practical for your clients.

Step 3: Market Research
Define Your Services Clearly

- Before starting your research, be clear about the specific services you offer. This could include program development, policy analysis, training workshops, etc. The more specific you are, the easier it will be to find comparable rates.

Identify Your Competitors
- Make a list of other public health consultants or consulting firms that offer similar services. Focus on those with a similar level of expertise and experience.
- Look for consultants who operate in a similar geographical area or target the same client base.

Gather Data on Pricing
- Check online resources: Many consultants and firms list their services and rates on their websites. Professional directories and platforms like LinkedIn can also be useful.
- Industry reports and surveys: Look for industry-specific reports or surveys that provide insights into average consulting rates. Organizations like the American Public Health Association (APHA) may publish relevant data.
- Freelance Marketplaces: Websites like Upwork or Fiverr can give you a sense of what freelancers in similar roles are charging, though these rates can sometimes be lower than standard consulting fees.

Conduct Informal Interviews
- Reach out to peers or mentors in the field for informational interviews. Ask them about their pricing strategies and what they've observed in the market.
- Attend networking events or webinars where you can casually gather insights about pricing from other professionals.

Analyze Job Postings and RFPs

- Review job postings or Requests for Proposals (RFPs) that are similar to the services you offer. These can sometimes include budget information or consultant rate expectations.

Consider the Scope of Work
- Remember that rates can vary significantly based on the project's scope, duration, and complexity. Factor these into your analysis.

Adjust for Your Unique Value Proposition
- Based on your unique skills and experiences, you may be able to command higher rates. Consider how your specific expertise adds value to your clients.

Document and Analyze Your Findings
- Keep a record of all the data you collect. Look for patterns and averages to determine a reasonable rate range for your services.

Stay Updated
- Market rates can change. Make it a habit to periodically revisit your research and adjust your rates accordingly.

Step 4: Choose a Pricing Model

Based on your services and market research, select a pricing model that best fits your business. Each pricing model has its advantages and challenges, and the choice depends on factors like the nature of your services, client preferences, and your business strategy. It's not uncommon for consultants to use a combination of these models, depending on the client and the type of project.

Hourly Rate
- You charge a set fee for each hour of work. This is straightforward for clients to understand.

- Best For: Projects where the scope is unclear or is expected to change. It's also suitable for ad-hoc or short-term consulting work.

Project-Based Fee
- A fixed fee is charged for the entire project, regardless of the time it takes. This fee is usually agreed upon after assessing the project's scope.
- Best For: Projects with a well-defined scope and deliverables. It's preferred by clients who want cost certainty.

Retainer
- Clients pay a regular, recurring fee (usually monthly) in exchange for access to your services over a period. This model ensures a steady income and client engagement.
- Best For: Long-term relationships where the client needs ongoing support, such as strategic advising or continuous project oversight.

Value-Based Pricing
- Fees are based on the value or outcome your consulting services provide to the client, rather than the time spent. This requires a deep understanding of the client's goals and the impact of your work.
- Best For: High-impact projects where your work directly contributes to significant client outcomes, like cost savings, revenue increase, or strategic transformation.

Performance-Based Pricing
- Part of your fee is tied to the achievement of specific results or performance metrics. This could be a bonus on top of a base fee or a contingent fee depending solely on performance.
- Best For: Projects where results are measurable and directly attributable to your consulting work, such as sales growth or efficiency improvements.

Day Rate (VIP Days)

Growing Your Public Health Consulting Business

- Like an hourly rate, but charges are based on a per-day basis. This is often used when a consultant works full days on a project.
- Best For: Intensive work that requires full days of commitment, like workshops, training sessions, or deep-dive analysis days.

Package Pricing
- Offering a bundle of services at a combined price, often at a discount compared to purchasing each service separately.
- Best For: When you have a suite of complementary services that can be packaged together, like a series of training modules or a combination of assessment, planning, and implementation services.

Step 5: Set Your Rates
Using the chosen model, set a preliminary rate for each service. Consider:
- Your experience and expertise.
- Market rates and client budgets.
- The complexity and scope of the work.
    - *Remember, it's okay if these are rough estimates for now.*

Step 6: Factor in Expenses and Desired Income
When setting consulting rates, it's essential to factor in business expenses (e.g., software, marketing, continuing education) to ensure profitability and sustainability. Here's a list of common business expenses that consultants often need to consider:

Office Expenses
- Rent: If you rent office space.

- Utilities: Electricity, water, internet, and phone bills.
- Office Supplies: Stationery, printer ink, paper, etc.

Technology Costs
- Hardware: Computers, printers, smartphones, and other necessary devices.
- Software Subscriptions: Licenses for specialized software, project management tools, accounting software, and other applications.

Professional Development
- Training and Certifications: Courses, workshops, and certifications to keep your skills and knowledge up to date.
- Conferences and Networking Events: Fees for attending industry events, which are crucial for networking and staying informed about industry trends.

Marketing and Advertising
- Website: Domain registration, hosting, design, and maintenance costs.
- Social media and Online Advertising: Costs associated with promoting your services online.
- Branding and Promotional Materials: Business cards, brochures, and other marketing materials.

Travel and Accommodation
- If your consulting work requires travel, include costs for transportation, hotels, meals, and other travel-related expenses.

Insurance
- Professional Liability Insurance: To protect against claims of negligence or harm.
- Health Insurance: If you're self-employed, you'll need to cover your health insurance.

Legal and Professional Fees
- Accounting Services: For managing business finances, taxes, and payroll (if applicable).
- Legal Services: For any legal advice, contract review, or business structure setup.

Membership and Subscription Fees
- Fees for professional associations, industry groups, or journals.

Taxes
- Setting aside a portion of income for taxes is crucial. The exact amount can vary based on your location and business structure.

Miscellaneous Expenses
- Unforeseen costs or miscellaneous purchases that support your business operations.

Step 7: Draft Your Pricing Structure
Create a simple table or list that outlines your services and their corresponding rates. Include any notes on discounts, package deals, or special conditions.

Step 8: Evaluate Your Pricing Structure
Evaluating your pricing structure is a critical aspect of ensuring the sustainability and growth of your consulting business. The pricing structure you set for your services should match your business model, provide value to clients, and generate sufficient revenue.

Step 9: Test Your Rates
Once you've set your rates, test them in the market. Be open to adjusting them based on client feedback and the success rate of your proposals. It's also crucial to understand the value of your work and not undervalue yourself. Remember, you are not just selling your time, but also your expertise and unique skill set. Therefore, it's important to factor in the value you bring to a project when determining your rates.

The Psychology of Pricing

Your mindset plays a critical role in pricing decisions and how clients perceive your value. Crafting a thoughtful pricing strategy that reflects your expertise and the market demand is essential. A growth mindset is needed to approach pricing with confidence, what I like to call the "compensation conversation". Pricing decisions are not easy to make, and it's natural to doubt your choices. However, having a growth mindset can help you overcome these doubts and approach pricing from a proactive perspective. Embracing the idea that you can always learn, adapt, and improve your pricing strategy can lead to better and more profitable pricing decisions. By considering these factors and trends, you can develop a pricing strategy that aligns with your expertise, market demands, and client expectations, ensuring a successful and sustainable consulting practice.

Packaging (Maximizing Your Brand)

Your brand is what sets you apart from the competition and helps you spark a connection with your audience. Your brand is what people will remember about you. When you first start your public health consulting business, you should spend a lot of time thinking about how you want your business represented. This includes defining your purpose, crafting your brand identity, and employing effective marketing strategies.

Defining Your Purpose: Mission, Vision, and Values

Creating a vision, mission, and values statement is a foundational step in defining the purpose, direction, and culture of your public health consulting business. These statements serve as a compass, guiding your business' actions, decisions, and interactions with clients, partners, and stakeholders, and they should resonate with your target audience and inspire trust and confidence in your business. Your Mission Statement is what your company is doing right now, while your Vision Statement is what you hope to achieve in the future – where you are in this moment versus where you're going. Sometimes the terms "Mission Statement" and "Vision Statement" are used interchangeably or even combined into a single statement. Your Values are a set of core values that reflect the principles and beliefs that guide your business. Values are clear and concise and align with the mission and vision of your business.

Mission
The mission is a concise statement that defines the fundamental purpose and primary objectives of an organization. It outlines what the organization does, who it serves, and how it achieves its goals. A mission statement serves as a guiding principle for the organization's activities and decision-making.

Mission Statement Formula
"Our mission is to [verb] [what] for [whom] [how]."
- Components

    o Verb: Use a strong action verb that reflects the core activities of your business.

    o What: Specify what your business does or provides.

    o For Whom: Define your target audience or the community you serve.

    o How: Describe the methods or approaches you use to achieve your mission.

Example: "Our mission is to provide access to quality healthcare for underserved communities through education and advocacy."

Vision
A vision statement is a forward-looking, aspirational statement that outlines the desired future state or long-term goals of an organization. It articulates what the organization hopes to achieve, the impact it aims to make, and the direction it is headed. A vision statement provides a sense

of purpose and inspiration for the organization's stakeholders.

Vision Statement Formula
"To [verb] [what] for [whom] [how] to achieve [why]."
- Components
    - Verb: Start with an action-oriented verb that describes what your business aims to do.
    - What: Describe what you want to accomplish or achieve.
    - For Whom: Identify the target audience or beneficiaries of your efforts.
    - How: Mention the approach or methods you will use.
    - Why: State the ultimate impact or purpose of your work.

Example: "Our vision is a world where every individual has equitable access to healthcare, leading to healthier communities and improved well-being."

Values
Values are a set of core principles and beliefs that guide the behavior, decisions, and culture of an organization. They represent the organization's ethical and moral framework and define the standards of conduct and professionalism it upholds. Values help shape the organization's identity and character.

Values Statement Formula
"At [Your Business Name], we are committed to [list of core values]."
Components:

- List a set of core values that reflect the principles and beliefs that guide your business.
- Keep the values concise and clear.
- Ensure they align with the mission and vision of your business.

Example Values:
- *Integrity: Upholding the highest ethical standards in all our interactions.*
- *Equity: Advocating for fair and just healthcare access for all.*
- *Innovation: Embracing creative solutions to public health challenges.*
- *Collaboration: Working together to achieve greater impact.*
- *Empowerment: Empowering individuals and communities to take control of their health.*

Tips for Creating Strong Statements
- Keep it concise and clear: Your statements should be easily understood and memorable.
- Reflect on your passion: Infuse your statements with your deep commitment to public health.
- Involve your team: Collaborate with your team to ensure everyone is aligned with the statements.
- Review and revise: Periodically revisit and update your statements to ensure they remain relevant and inspiring.

Crafting Your Brand Identity

Your brand identity is the visible elements of your brand, such as the colors, designs, and logo, that identify and distinguish the brand in consumers' minds. Branding is important for brand awareness (recognition), building trust and customer loyalty, and building credibility (this is the know, like, trust factor I mentioned earlier). When it comes to branding, the key is to get it right the first time because rebranding is timely and costly (Trust me). Your brand identity is the first impression that a customer has of your company. It is what makes your brand unique and memorable, setting it apart from your competitors. Therefore, it is essential to carefully plan and create a strong brand identity that resonates with your target audience.

Below are the most crucial elements of your brand identity:

Logo
A logo is a visual symbol or design that represents an organization, brand, or product. It is a distinctive and recognizable image that often includes unique shapes, colors, and typography. Logos are used for branding and marketing purposes to create visual identity and recognition.

Example: The Nike "Swoosh" logo

Slogan/Tagline
A slogan or tagline is a short and memorable phrase or sentence that conveys the essence of a brand, product, or organization. It is used in marketing and advertising to capture the attention of the audience and communicate key messages or values succinctly.

Example: Nike's "Just Do It"

Colors

Colors in branding refer to the specific hues and color palette chosen to represent an organization. Colors can evoke emotions, convey brand personality, and create visual consistency. They play a crucial role in brand recognition and identity.

Example: Coca-Cola's signature red color

Typography (Fonts)

Typography refers to the choice and arrangement of fonts (typefaces) used in visual communication, including branding, marketing materials, and publications. Different fonts have distinct styles and characteristics, impacting the overall look and feel of design. Consistent typography contributes to brand identity.

Example: The use of the "Helvetica" font in Apple's branding

Imagery

Description: Imagery includes visual elements such as photographs, illustrations, graphics, and icons used to convey messages and enhance communication. In branding, imagery should align with the brand's values and messaging and contribute to the overall visual identity.

Example: The use of images of happy families in advertisements for a family-oriented healthcare organization

Messaging

Messaging encompasses the words, language, and content used to communicate an organization's values, mission, products, or services to its target audience. Effective messaging should be clear, consistent, and aligned with the brand's identity and objectives. It plays a vital role in marketing and communication strategies.

Example: A healthcare organization's messaging highlighting its commitment to patient-centered care and preventive health measures

Offline and Online Marketing Strategies

As technology continues to evolve, the marketing landscape has also drastically changed. In today's digital age, businesses have endless opportunities to reach their target audience through various online platforms and the use of offline and online marketing. Offline marketing is any form of marketing that does not involve the use of digital technologies. This can include traditional forms such as print ads, billboards, and television commercials. Online marketing is an important aspect of digital marketing which aims to promote products and services through online platforms. While offline marketing may seem outdated in comparison to online methods, it still holds a significant place in the overall marketing strategy of businesses.

Offline marketing allows businesses to reach potential customers who may not have access to or prefer not to use digital media. For example, print ads in local newspapers can be effective for reaching a target audience that is not active online or uses traditional methods of obtaining information. Examples of offline marketing include:

- Events and workshops
- Speaking engagements
- Networking events
- Vendor/sponsor
- Flyers
- Business cards

Online marketing has become increasingly popular in recent years due to the growth of the internet and the use of digital devices. With more people spending time online, businesses have recognized the importance of establishing a strong online presence to reach potential customers. One of the main advantages of online marketing is its ability to target specific audiences. Through methods like search engine optimization and paid advertising, businesses can tailor their marketing efforts to reach people who are most likely interested in their products or services. This allows for a more efficient use of resources and a higher return on investment. Online marketing is more effective than offline marketing as far as reach, effort, and cost. It's also much easier to track results and referrals using online marketing. Some examples of online marketing include:

- Email marketing
- Social media marketing
- SEO optimization
- Paid advertising
- Influencer marketing
- Affiliate marketing
- Podcasts

Social Media Marketing
Before I discuss the benefits of social media marketing for your business, let me provide this disclaimer. I know several successful public health consultants who are not active on social media. I even know public health consultants that don't even have websites. Your business model is yours to decide. I am not trying to insinuate that social media is the only way to promote yourself as a public health consultant. However, it can be an incredibly useful tool for doing so. With that being said, let's dive into why social media marketing is crucial for your business.

Social media marketing allows you to reach a larger audience at a lower cost compared to traditional marketing methods. With billions of active users on various social media platforms, you have the potential to connect with a vast number of individuals who may be interested in your services or products. Secondly, social media allows for targeted advertising, which means you can tailor your marketing efforts to reach a specific demographic. This not only saves money but also ensures that your message is reaching the right audience. Additionally, social media allows for real-time engagement with your audience. This means you can quickly respond to comments, answer questions, and address any concerns or issues from prospects, clients, and partners. This level of interaction helps build trust and credibility with your audience, ultimately leading to customer loyalty and increased sales.

Another benefit of social media marketing is its ability to generate valuable insights and data about your audience. Through various analytics tools, you can track the performance of your posts, measure engagement, and gather information about your followers' demographics and interests. This data can then be used to refine your marketing strategy and make informed decisions to further improve your business. In addition to these benefits, social media also allows for easy collaboration and partnerships with other businesses or influencers. By teaming up with others in your industry, you can reach a wider audience and tap into new markets. Collaborations also help to enhance your brand's credibility and establish it as an authority within your niche.

Social Media Platforms
The best social media platform for your business depends on various factors, including your target audience, the type of content you plan to share, and your business goals. To decide which platform is best for your business, consider your target audience demographics, the type of content you

plan to create, and your business objectives. You may also want to research your competitors' presence on different platforms and analyze which platforms are most effective for reaching your target audience. Additionally, you should consider starting out with only one or two platforms initially to focus your efforts and resources effectively. Below are some popular social media platforms and considerations for each.

Facebook
Audience: Wide-ranging demographics, including users of all ages.
Content: Suitable for various types of content, including text posts, images, videos, and live streams.
Business Goals: Effective for building brand awareness, engaging with customers, and driving website traffic.

Instagram
Audience: Primarily younger demographics, especially millennials and Gen Z.
Content: Visual-focused platform ideal for sharing high-quality images and short videos.
Business Goals: Great for showcasing products/services, building a visually appealing brand identity, and reaching a highly engaged audience.

X (formerly known as Twitter)
Audience: Broad range of demographics, with a focus on news, trends, and real-time communication.
Content: Short-form text posts (tweets), images, videos, and links.
Business Goals: Useful for sharing timely updates, engaging in conversations with customers, and driving website traffic through links.

LinkedIn
Audience: Professionals, businesses, and job seekers.

Content: Professional and business-related content, including articles, industry news, and job postings.
Business Goals: Effective for networking, establishing thought leadership, generating leads, and recruiting talent.

Pinterest
Audience: Predominantly female users interested in lifestyle, DIY, fashion, and home decor.
Content: A highly visual platform for sharing images and videos (pins) organized by categories.
Business Goals: Ideal for showcasing products/services, driving website traffic, and reaching users in the consideration phase of the purchase journey.

YouTube
Audience: Broad range of demographics, with a focus on video content.
Content: Video-based platform for sharing tutorials, product demos, vlogs, and entertainment.
Business Goals: Effective for building brand awareness, demonstrating products/services, and engaging with audiences through video content.

TikTok
Audience: Primarily younger demographics, especially Gen Z.
Content: Short-form vertical videos, often with music and creative effects.
Business Goals: Ideal for reaching a younger audience, showcasing creativity, and generating viral content.

To conclude, social media marketing has numerous benefits for businesses looking to enhance their online presence and reach a wider audience. By utilizing its various tools and features, you can build trust with your audience, gather valuable insights, communicate directly with customers, collaborate with others, and promote your brand at a low cost. As the digital landscape continues to evolve, it will be crucial for businesses to embrace social media as a powerful marketing tool to maximize their brand and scale their business.

Chapter 10:
Scaling Your Public Health Business

Introduction
To scale in business means that your revenue and capacity increase without a substantial increase in resources. This phase of business involves streamlining your business processes, improving your client experience, incorporating business tools and technology, growing your team, and becoming more comfortable with pitching your services to potential clients.

Processes (Minimize and Optimize Your Processes)
Streamlining your business processes is crucial for scaling a public health venture effectively. This involves finding the right balance between your team, the tools they use, and the tasks they handle. The initial step in minimizing and optimizing your processes is to evaluate each task's impact on your goals, efficiency, and overall value. From there, prioritize the automation, delegation, and elimination of tasks within your consulting business. Through strategic implementation of these approaches, you can streamline your business processes and dedicate more time to high-impact activities that drive your business forward. These activities include the creation of workflow automation, as well as the incorporation of business tools and technology.

Automation
Automation saves you time, hassle, and worry. You may be new to this term, but chances are you are already automating some things. If you are busy and you let your phone calls go to voicemail, that's automation. If your monthly bills are set up on autopay so you don't have to worry about making the payment, that's automation. Automation works just as well in your business as it does in your personal life. Just set, schedule, and forget it! (Well, sort of). By automating certain tasks and processes, you can save time, reduce manual

errors, enhance client interactions, and focus on the core activities that drive your consulting business forward. Automation can significantly improve efficiency and help you deliver better results to your clients. Examples of tasks that can be automated in your business include:

- Email Marketing: Use email marketing platforms to automate client communication, newsletters, and updates.

- Appointment Scheduling: Implement scheduling software that allows clients to book appointments at their convenience.

- Social Media Posting: Schedule social media posts in advance using tools like Hootsuite or Buffer.

- Invoicing and Payment: Use accounting software to automate invoicing and payment reminders.

- Client Onboarding: Create automated onboarding sequences that provide new clients with welcome messages, access to resources, and important information about your consulting services.

- Data Collection and Analysis: Use online forms or surveys to collect data from clients or stakeholders. Responses can be automatically organized and analyzed using data analytics tools.

- Task Management: Implement project management software to automate task assignments, deadlines, and progress tracking among your team members or collaborators.

- Expense Tracking: Use expense management software to automate the tracking and categorization of business expenses, making financial management more efficient.

Delegation

Let me tell you from experience - burnout is the result of not delegating. You MUST delegate, and not just at work or in your business. Delegate at home by asking for help. Delegate in your business by hiring help! Delegating requires you to get comfortable with giving less important tasks to others so you can save the higher-priority tasks for yourself. Delegating tasks in a consulting business can help you leverage the skills and expertise of others while allowing you to focus on higher-value activities that contribute to the growth and success of your consulting business, enabling you to scale your operations and better serve your clients. Here are some examples of things that can often be delegated:

- Content Creation: Delegate writing blog posts, articles, or content for marketing materials to freelance writers or content creators.

- Social Media Management: Hire a social media manager to handle content creation, posting, and engagement on your social media platforms.

- Administrative Tasks: Employ virtual assistants to manage administrative duties like email management, appointment scheduling, and travel arrangements.

- Graphic Design: Outsource graphic design tasks such as creating visual materials for presentations, reports, or marketing collateral.

- Website Maintenance: Delegate website updates, maintenance, and improvements to a web developer or designer.

- Project Management: Appoint a project manager to oversee project timelines, task assignments, and progress tracking.

- Legal and Compliance Matters: Consult with legal professionals or compliance experts for legal advice, contracts, and regulatory compliance.

- IT and Technical Support: Outsource IT support or technical assistance to ensure that your technology infrastructure runs smoothly.

- Sales and Business Development: If you have a sales team, delegate lead generation, client acquisition, and relationship management to them.

- Bookkeeping and Accounting: Hire an accountant or use accounting services to manage financial records, expenses, and tax filings.

Elimination

You can automate and delegate as much as you want to but at some point, you're just going to have to take some things off your plate. You can't eliminate all the areas in your life and business, but you can eliminate what's not necessary. Consider Pareto's Principle, also known as the 80/20 rule. Chances are 80% of your success is coming from 20% of your effort. Prioritize the 20% and eliminate the rest. Eliminating non-essential or redundant elements in your consulting business can free up valuable time, reduce operational costs, and allow you to focus on activities that generate revenue, deliver value to clients, and contribute to the growth and success of your consultancy. Examples of things in your business that can be eliminated:

- Non-Value-Adding Meetings: Eliminate meetings that do not contribute to the growth or progress of your consulting business.

- Manual Data Entry: Reduce manual data entry by implementing tools that can capture data automatically.

- Redundant Administrative Tasks: Identify and eliminate repetitive administrative tasks that can be streamlined.

- Unprofitable Projects: Don't hesitate to drop projects that are not financially viable or do not align with your expertise.

- Low-Value Clients: Identify clients who consistently require extensive time and resources but yield low returns. Consider whether it's worth continuing these relationships.

- Non-Essential Software or Tools: Evaluate the software and tools you use in your consulting business. Eliminate those that are redundant or no longer serve a crucial purpose.

- Non-Strategic Networking: Be selective in your networking efforts. Focus on relationships and events that align with your consulting niche and goals and eliminate those that do not.

- Unproductive Partnerships: Reevaluate partnerships or collaborations that are not mutually beneficial or do not align with your consulting business' long-term goals.

Business Workflow Creation

Automation refers to the use of technology and systems to perform tasks, processes, or operations with minimal human intervention. It involves the implementation of software or hardware systems to streamline workflows, increase efficiency, and reduce manual effort in completing repetitive or routine tasks. Your business needs automation to scale while reducing costs, errors, and reliance on manual labor. Automation plays a crucial role in modern business operations, allowing companies to focus on higher-value activities, innovation, and strategic decision-making.

Workflow Automation defines a sequence of steps, actions, and decisions required to complete a specific process or task. Software Automation uses software applications or scripts to automate tasks such as data analysis, email marketing, or customer relationship management. Several workflows can be automated in your business to streamline various aspects of the client and improve your clients' experience. By implementing workflow automation, businesses can enhance efficiency, improve communication, and provide a seamless experience for clients, students, staff, and collaborating partners. Below are samples of workflows that can (and should be) automated in your business.

Inquiry Workflow
Trigger: Prospect submits an inquiry form on the website.
Action: Automated email response: Send a personalized acknowledgment email thanking the client for their inquiry and providing an estimated response time.
Task creation: Create a task in the CRM system to follow up on the inquiry.
Follow-up: Assign the task to the appropriate team member for further action.

Scheduling/Booking Workflow
Trigger: The Prospect requests a consultation or service appointment.
Action 1: Automated scheduling link: Provide Prospect with a link to your online scheduling system where they can select an available time slot.
Action 2: Confirmation email: Automatically send a confirmation email with the appointment details once the booking is confirmed.
Follow-up: Send a reminder email or text message closer to the appointment date.

Contracts/Invoices Workflow
Trigger: A service agreement is reached with the client.
Action 1: Automated contract generation: Generate a customized contract template with the client's details using document automation software.
Action 2: Electronic signature: Send the contract electronically for the client to sign using an e-signature tool.
Action 3: Automatically generate and send the invoice for the agreed-upon services.
Follow-up: Set up automated payment reminders for overdue invoices.

Onboarding Workflow
Trigger: The Client signs the contract and pays the invoice.
Action 1: Welcome package: Automatically send a welcome email with onboarding instructions, resources, and next steps.
Action 2: Onboarding checklist: Create a checklist of tasks for the client to complete, such as filling out intake forms or attending orientation sessions.
Action 3: Assigned staff: Assign a staff member or mentor to guide the client through the onboarding process.
Follow-up: Monitor progress and send automated check-in emails to ensure a smooth onboarding experience.

Projects/Services Workflow
Trigger: The onboarding process is completed.
Action 1: Project setup: Automatically create project folders, assign tasks, and set deadlines using project management software.
Action 2: Progress updates: Automatically send periodic progress updates to the client, detailing milestones achieved and next steps.
Task: Set up automated reminders for upcoming tasks or deliverables.
Follow-up: Schedule regular check-in meetings to discuss progress and address any concerns.

Events Workflow
Trigger: Event registration is confirmed.
Action 1: Event details: Automatically send event details, including date, time, location, and agenda, to registered attendees.
Action 2: Event reminders: Send automated reminders leading up to the event to ensure attendance.
Action 3: Post-event follow-up: Automatically send a thank-you email to attendees and gather feedback through automated surveys.
Follow-up: Analyze event metrics and use insights to improve future events.

Business Tools and Technology

Incorporating various business tools and technologies is vital in scaling your public health consulting business. These tools enhance efficiency, productivity, communication, and collaboration within organizations, and cater to various aspects of business operations, marketing, sales, and customer engagement. There are various tools and platforms that you can use in your business. Several examples are listed below.

Accounting Software
Accounting software helps businesses manage financial transactions, track expenses, create invoices, and generate financial reports.
Examples: QuickBooks, FreshBooks, Wave, Zoho Books

Customer Relationship Management (CRM) Software
CRM software enables businesses to manage interactions with current and potential customers, track leads, automate sales processes, and analyze customer data.
Examples: HoneyBook, 17hats, Dubsado, Salesforce

Project/Task Management Software
Project/task management software assists in organizing and prioritizing tasks, assigning responsibilities, setting deadlines, and tracking project progress.
Examples: Asana, Trello, Monday.com, ClickUp

Proposal Developer
Proposal development software helps businesses create professional proposals, quotes, and contracts for clients, streamlining the sales process.
Examples: Better Proposals, PandaDoc, Proposify

Scheduling Software
Scheduling software simplifies appointment scheduling, allowing clients or team members to book appointments online based on availability.
Examples: Calendly, Acuity Scheduling, Book Like A Boss

Screen and Video Recording Software
Screen/video recording software enables users to capture their computer screen or record videos for tutorials, presentations, or demonstrations.
Examples: Loom, Free Cam, Screencast-O-Matic, Zoom

Time Tracking Software
Time tracking software helps businesses monitor and record the time spent on various tasks and projects, facilitating accurate billing and productivity analysis.
Examples: Clockify, Harvest, Toggl, Hubstaff, Quickbooks Time

Video Conferencing
Video conferencing software allows users to conduct virtual meetings, webinars, and online presentations with participants from different locations.
Examples: Zoom, Microsoft Teams, GoToMeeting, BlueJeans, Google Meet

Websites
Website-building platforms enable businesses to create and customize their websites without extensive coding knowledge, providing a digital presence for their brand.
Examples: Zenler, Squarespace, Wix, GoDaddy Website Builder, WordPress

Email Software
Email marketing software helps businesses design, send, and track email campaigns, manage subscriber lists, and analyze campaign performance.
Examples: Mailchimp, MailerLite, Constant Contact, ConvertKit

Social Media Scheduling Software
Social media scheduling software allows businesses to plan, schedule, and publish content across multiple social media platforms in advance, saving time and maintaining a consistent presence.
Examples: Hootsuite, Buffer, Planable, PromoRepublic, Later

Content Development Software
Content development software provides tools for creating and editing visual content, such as graphics, presentations, infographics, and videos, to support marketing and communication efforts.
Examples: Canva, Adobe Creative Cloud, Venngage

Scripted Business Templates
A secret weapon in business automation is the use of scripted business templates. Having pre-developed scripts in your business can significantly improve efficiency, consistency, and professionalism in various interactions with clients, customers, and stakeholders. Having these scripts ready saves time, ensures consistency in communication, and empowers your team to handle various situations confidently and professionally. Below are some common scripts that can be beneficial to have pre-prepared. Keep in mind these scripts are even more efficient when utilized with a CRM.

- ***Introduction Script***: A concise script to introduce yourself or your company when initiating contact with a new prospect or client.

- ***Sales Script:*** A structured script outlining key points and persuasive language to guide sales conversations and pitch your products or services effectively.

- ***Cold Calling Script:*** A script to follow when making cold calls to potential leads or clients, including opening lines, value propositions, and responses to common objections.

- ***Follow-up Script:*** Templates for follow-up emails or calls after initial contact or meetings, reinforcing key points, addressing concerns, and moving the conversation forward.

- ***Customer Service Script***: Scripts for handling common customer inquiries, complaints, or requests, ensuring consistent and helpful responses from your team.

- **Appointment Confirmation Script**: A script to confirm appointments with clients or customers, including details such as date, time, location, and any required preparations.

- **Feedback Request Script:** Templates for soliciting feedback from clients or customers after completing a project, purchase, or service, encouraging honest input and suggestions for improvement.

- **Referral Request Script:** A script to ask satisfied clients or customers for referrals to potential new business opportunities, emphasizing the value of their recommendations.

- **Invoice Reminder Script:** Templates for sending polite reminders to clients about outstanding invoices, encouraging prompt payment while maintaining a positive relationship.

- **Social Media Response Script:** Guidelines for responding to comments, messages, or reviews on social media platforms, ensuring timely and professional interactions with your audience.

- **Networking Script:** A script to use when introducing yourself at networking events or meetings, highlighting your expertise, interests, and potential collaboration opportunities.

- **Onboarding Script:** Scripts or guides for welcoming new clients or customers onboard, providing essential information, setting expectations, and explaining the next steps.

- **Employee Training Scripts:** Scripts or training materials for teaching employees how to handle specific tasks, interactions, or scenarios effectively and consistently.

- **Thank-You Script:** Templates for sending personalized thank-you messages or notes to clients, customers, partners, or team members, expressing appreciation for their support or collaboration.

Growing Your Team

Hiring new team members can be a daunting and expensive task for any business, but especially for small businesses and startups. Many entrepreneurs choose to do it all by themselves in the beginning, wearing multiple hats and taking on every task that needs to be done. While this may seem like the most cost-effective approach, it can hinder your growth potential in the long run. Here's my advice: Hire help before you think you can afford it! Even if that means you take a cut in your pay.

By bringing in new team members, you can delegate tasks and free up more time to focus on the bigger picture of growing your business. This will also allow you to scale your operations and take on more clients or projects without feeling overwhelmed. Furthermore, having a diverse team with different skills and perspectives can bring fresh ideas and solutions to the table and allow you to take on bigger and more complex projects that you may not have been able to handle alone. By expanding your team, you can achieve bigger dreams for your business. Below are five tips for hiring help to support your public health consulting business even if you're operating on a limited budget.

1. *Start with freelancers or contractors:* Hiring freelancers or contractors on a project basis allows you to access specialized skills without committing to full-time salaries.

2. *Utilize interns or volunteers:* Consider bringing on interns or volunteers who are eager to gain experience in public health.

This can provide them with valuable learning opportunities while helping you with tasks that don't require full-time staff.

3. *Outsource non-core functions:* Identify tasks or functions that are not core to your business and consider outsourcing them to third-party providers. This can free up your time to focus on growing your business and serving your clients.

4. *Network and collaborate*: Build relationships with other consultants or professionals in the public health field who may be able to provide support or referrals. Collaborating with others can help you expand your reach and capabilities without hiring additional staff.

5. *Prioritize tasks and responsibilities:* Focus on hiring help for tasks that are essential for scaling your business and generating revenue. Prioritize roles that directly contribute to your business growth and client satisfaction.

Pitching (Making Money)
Trust me, I get it. Selling your services and convincing someone to do business with you can feel daunting, especially in the beginning. When I first started my business, I struggled with the idea of asking people to invest their hard-earned money in what I had to offer. After all, I had spent so many years giving away my expertise for free that it felt uncomfortable to attach a price tag to it. But here's the truth: if you're not making money in business, then you're not really in business at all. You're just running an expensive and time-consuming hobby. Unfortunately, many public health consultants find themselves in this position when trying to launch their businesses.

The key to success in sales is to reframe how you think about the sales process. Instead of viewing it as "selling," think of it as "serving" and providing a valuable service to your clients. Your clients have a problem and your expertise and solutions are exactly what they need to solve their problems and achieve their goals. By approaching sales from this perspective, you'll feel more confident and comfortable pitching your services and ultimately, scaling your public health consulting business.

Pitching public health consulting services to potential clients requires a thoughtful and persuasive approach. To communicate effectively in your pitch, you need to have a deep understanding of the client's needs and a focus on delivering tangible results. Tailoring your approach and demonstrating the value you bring will greatly increase your chances of winning clients and making a positive impact in the field of public health. Let's review the different ways that public health consultants actually make money.

Pitches
The proactive way to make money as a public health entrepreneur is to sell (or pitch) your services and products. Many public health consultants run their business solely on "word-of-mouth" marketing and while this can seem like a safe bet, it limits the potential for you to scale your business due to limited reach and the unpredictability of a referral-based business. While word-of-mouth referrals can be a valuable source of business, it's important to complement this approach with other marketing tactics such as networking, content marketing, social media, and targeted advertising. By diversifying your client acquisition strategies, you can reach a broader audience, attract new clients, and ensure the long-term sustainability of your public health consulting business. I pitch my solutions to my ideal clients every single day. I provide discovery calls, I give sales presentations, and I nurture my business leads because the fortune is in the follow-up. The key to pitching your consulting solutions is to know your prospect and tailor your pitch accordingly. This means understanding their pain points, needs, and how your services can specifically help them. There are several different ways that you can pitch your services including:

<u>Pitching through Email</u>
Email is a popular method for pitching because it allows you to reach out directly to potential clients without any interruptions. When crafting an email pitch, make sure to keep it concise

and clear. Introduce yourself briefly and explain why you are reaching out to them. Then, highlight the benefits of your services and how they can solve their problems. You can also include any relevant case studies or success stories to showcase your expertise and credibility. Make sure to personalize each email pitch according to the recipient's needs and interests.

Pitching through LinkedIn messaging
LinkedIn is a valuable platform for making professional connections and pitching your services. Similar to email pitches, make sure to introduce yourself and explain why you are reaching out. Use the messaging feature to personalize your pitch and show genuine interest in the recipient's business. You can also use LinkedIn to research potential clients and tailor your pitch accordingly. Join relevant groups and participate in discussions related to public health entrepreneurship to expand your network.

Pitching through Phone calls
Cold calling can be intimidating, but it can also be an effective way to pitch your services. Before making the call, research the company and its needs to tailor your pitch accordingly. Make sure to have a clear and concise script prepared. Warm outreach through phone calls involves reaching out to clients who have shown interest in your services or have been referred to you. This approach can be more successful as the potential client has already shown some level of interest in what you have to offer.

Pitching through Social Media
In addition to pitching through traditional methods, it's important to utilize social media platforms such as Facebook and Instagram to showcase your services and engage with potential clients. Share updates about your business, relevant industry news, and interact with followers to build a strong online presence.

Pitching at In-person Events
Networking events and conferences are also great opportunities to pitch your services. These events allow you to connect with individuals in the public health industry and promote your business face-to-face. Make sure to have an elevator pitch prepared and exchange contact information with potential clients.

The Art of Pitching Your Services
To effectively engage potential clients and secure projects, it's essential to first thoroughly understand their client's needs. This involves researching their organization to grasp the specific public health challenges they face, their organizational goals, and identifying where your expertise can significantly impact their pain points and areas of need. Crafting a compelling pitch is crucial; it should be concise, engaging, and articulate who you are, your expertise, and the unique value you bring to the table, focusing on the outcomes and benefits of your services. By focusing on the results, you can showcase how your services will impact their bottom line and contribute to their overall success. Clients want to work with consultants who are knowledgeable, reliable, and have a proven track record of delivering results. They want to see evidence of past successes, relevant experience, and knowledge in the field of public health.

Lastly, when pitching to clients, it's crucial to have a clear understanding of their budget and resources. Public health consulting can involve significant financial investments, so it's important to clearly communicate the cost-benefit of your services. This way, clients can see the value in investing in your expertise and feel confident that their resources will be put to good use. By mastering these skills, you can increase your chances of securing new clients, scaling a sustainable business, and making a positive impact in the field of public health.

Business Proposals
A business proposal is how you sell yourself and your company's capabilities on paper. It is a document that outlines

your products or services, and how they can benefit another business or organization. Business proposals are essential for securing new clients, partnerships, and funding opportunities. The opportunity to draft a business proposal usually comes after an initial discussion like a discovery call. The most common components of a business proposal include an executive summary, company background and qualifications, fees and pricing structure, and terms and conditions. Perhaps the most important part of a business proposal for public health consultants is the Scope of Work (SOW). The SOW section of a business proposal is crucial because it clearly defines what the project will entail, what deliverables are expected, and the specific tasks or services to be provided. This section sets the boundaries and expectations for both the client and the service provider, ensuring there is a mutual understanding of the project's extent and limitations. A well-defined SOW is essential for the success of any project. It helps in preventing misunderstandings, managing client expectations, and providing a clear roadmap for project execution. It serves as a reference point for both parties and can be crucial in resolving disputes or clarifications. By detailing exactly what is to be done, how, by whom, and by when, it lays the foundation for a successful partnership and project outcome. Below are the components of a Scope of Work.

Project Overview
- Begins with a brief description of the project, including its purpose and the problem it aims to solve or the need it intends to meet.

- Objectives: Outlines the primary goals of the project, providing a clear picture of the desired outcome.

Deliverables
- List of Deliverables: Specifies the tangible or intangible products to be delivered upon project completion, such as reports, plans, software, training sessions, or research findings.

- Delivery Timeline: Includes deadlines for each deliverable, offering a schedule that aligns with the project's overall timeline.

Scope Details
- Tasks and Services: Details of the specific tasks to be performed or services provided. This can include stages of work, methodologies to be used, and any phases or milestones within the project.
- Exclusions: Clearly states what is not included in the project scope, helping to manage client expectations and prevent scope creep.

Project Milestones and Timeline
- Milestones: Identifies key milestones within the project, including major phases, decision points, or events that signify progress.
- Overall Timeline: Provides an estimated timeline for the project, from start to finish, including the duration of each phase or task.

Resources and Staffing
- Team Composition: Describes the team members or roles required to complete the project, including any specific expertise or qualifications.
- Resource Allocation: Outlines the resources (human, technological, financial) allocated to each part of the project.

Contracts

The right contract can carry your public health consulting business for months. But they are not always easy to secure. It took me 18 months of responding to Request for Proposals (RFPs) to land my first contract. An RFP is a formal invitation to submit a proposal for public health consulting services. An effective way to increase your chances of winning an RFP is to position yourself as an expert in the specific area that the contract requires. This means doing extensive research on the client's needs, understanding their goals and objectives, and tailoring your proposal accordingly. And even then, success is not guaranteed. Here are some things to consider when it comes to government contracts:

- There can be a huge time investment in writing an RFP.
- There is usually a large number of organizations competing for the same opportunity which lowers your odds of winning the bid.
- You can enhance the likelihood of success by partnering with another consultant or organization.
- Relying solely on responding to RFPs as a business model is not advisable. A more robust approach involves diversifying income sources to create multiple revenue streams.

Multiple Streams of Revenue
As an entrepreneur, it's crucial to have multiple streams of income to ensure the long-term success and sustainability of your company. Relying on just one source of revenue can be risky, as unexpected changes in the market or economy can greatly impact your business. Having multiple sources of income can help mitigate these risks and provide a stable foundation for your consulting business. For example, in addition to providing consulting, training, and technical assistance to organizations, my public health consultancy also generates revenue by selling continuing education courses, licensing our CHW training curriculum, selling digital products like workbooks and toolkits, and booking speaking engagements. These are things that I refer to as our complimentary consulting services.

Having to rely on a single source of income can make your consulting business vulnerable to economic fluctuations, client changes, or unexpected disruptions. Multiple income streams provide a safety net, helping you weather financial challenges more effectively. Diversifying your income reduces dependence on a single client or revenue source, spreading the risk. Multiple streams of income also significantly increase your overall revenue potential because different income streams come from various sources. Each income source contributes to your bottom line, allowing you to earn more and achieve financial goals faster.

Chapter 11:
Purpose and Profit: Balancing Your Bottom Line with Your Higher Calling

Introduction
If you've been reading up to this point, I extend my heartfelt gratitude for joining me on this journey. I trust that it has been both an enlightening and transformative experience for you. And now, as we draw near the end of this book, I offer you a warm welcome. Welcome to the intersection of purpose and profit, where your bottom line meets your higher calling. At this intersection, it's not about prioritizing one over the other but balancing them equally —to ensure that the pursuit of profit amplifies the pursuit of your purpose. The journey of the public health entrepreneur is one fueled by purpose, sustained by profit, and driven by a relentless commitment to creating a healthier, equitable world where when purpose and profit converge, they become formidable allies, transforming lives and communities alike.

Defining Purpose and Profit in the Context of Business
Becoming a public health entrepreneur means you will perform a balancing act where the pursuit of societal well-being merges with the world of business. This is not a place where many people feel comfortable. That's why entrepreneurship is not for everyone. However, if you allow yourself to step outside of your comfort zone, you will find a place where purpose and profit seamlessly intertwine and co-exist. You've probably heard the saying before: "there are two sides to every coin." Well, entrepreneurship is a two-sided coin. Every day, you take the good with the bad, but every day you will also have

the best of both worlds. Before I go deeper into this chapter, let me establish how I define purpose and profit in the context of business.

For me, to be **'Purpose-Driven'** is to be guided by a deep sense of meaning, mission, or core values that go beyond financial gain or external recognition. It involves a strong commitment to a higher purpose or a set of principles that serve as the foundation for one's actions and decisions.

To be **'Profit-Focused'** is to prioritize profitability to ensure long-term viability. It means placing a strong emphasis on generating revenue, maximizing profitability, and achieving financial freedom, all while striking a balance between profit-focused goals and social responsibility to achieve sustainable success.

The Importance of Purpose in Public Health Entrepreneurship
For public health entrepreneurs, purpose is the North Star that guides their journey. It's the unwavering commitment to improving the health and well-being of individuals and communities. Purpose infuses their work with passion, meaning, and a profound sense of duty. You do not want to become a public health entrepreneur if you don't have a purpose. In fact, I would argue that you wouldn't be happy or successful if your sole goal in starting a business was only to make a profit. However, to be successful in this field, it is important to find a balance between the two.

The first step in finding that balance is to have a clear understanding of your purpose and values as an entrepreneur. What motivates you? What are your goals beyond financial gain? How do you want to contribute to society? Purpose-driven entrepreneurs, especially those who work in public health, understand that their mission transcends the bank account. They recognize that their actions ripple through communities, shaping the health and lives of those they serve. Purpose becomes the driving force behind innovative solutions, the catalyst for addressing health disparities, as well as the foundation of their brand.

Once you have a strong sense of your purpose, it is important to align your business model with it. This means considering the potential social impact of your products or services, as well as the financial viability of your business. It may require making difficult decisions and trade-offs, but ultimately, it will allow you to stay true to your higher calling while also ensuring the success of your business.

The Role of Profit in Sustainability
While purpose ignites the spark, profit fuels the engine of sustainable impact. When it comes to public health entrepreneurship, profit is not a dirty word. I repeat, profit is not a dirty word. As much as we may want to believe that businesses and organizations operate solely for the greater good, they don't! And, if they do, they won't be around long enough to make an impact. Profit is a crucial component in creating sustainable impact. Profit (making money) is what allows organizations to keep the doors open. Profit is the main driving force behind sustainability efforts. Period! However, for sustainability to be realized and to make a lasting impact, every facet of your business must be in alignment with its purpose and values. This is where the concept of being "purpose-driven, profit-focused" comes into play. Public health entrepreneurs must have a strong commitment to their

purpose while prioritizing their profitability. And in order to be profitable, you have to charge for your services.

The Fear of Charging for Good Deeds

Here is the honest truth: *Helping professionals* have a difficult time charging others for their services. Many fear that charging for the good they do might somehow diminish their altruism, taint their intentions, or alienate those in need. In fact, I interviewed a potential co-author for this book and her reply was *"having my story (and business) featured in a book with the word "profit" in the title isn't the image that I want to project for my business."* She verbalized to me during our meeting that she was afraid that the nonprofit organizations that she works with would get the wrong impression about her and think that she was only "in it for the money".

In reality, the ability to charge for services is not a contradiction but a necessity. Charging appropriately for services allows you as a public health entrepreneur to sustain your work and expand your reach. It enables you to dedicate more time and resources to your mission, ultimately benefiting the individuals, communities, and organizations that you serve. When you charge appropriately and your business is profitable, you can scale innovative business ventures without constraint because you have the resources you need to invest in business development, outreach, and more. Profitability secures the future of your initiatives, ensuring they are not fleeting endeavors but enduring forces for change. If you are reading this book, I'm giving you permission to charge for your working experience and expertise, as well as your lived experience, as they are all necessary and required for the pursuit of health equity.

Purpose and Profit: Balancing Your Bottom Line with Your Higher Calling

Yes, it's okay for you to charge for expertise related to your lived experience. Your lived experience can inform and improve systems, research, policies, practices, and programs.

Yes, it's okay for you to charge to do something you love doing anyway. If you charge, you won't get burnt out and you can continue doing it.

Yes, it's okay for you to charge to do something that comes easily to you. It didn't at one point! It's a benefit to your clients if you can do in one hour what takes someone else an entire day.

Here's what I'm trying to say. You took out loans, got degrees and certifications, put in long hours to learn what you know now and have lived a full life of experiences that can provide insight into matters that individuals, communities, and organizations may find insightful and just what they need in their next public health consultant. Own it. Embrace it. Charge for it!

Balancing Purpose and Profit: A Delicate Dance
The art of public health entrepreneurship lies in the delicate dance between purpose and profit. It's a balance that requires thoughtful consideration and continuous reflection. The aim is not to prioritize one over the other but to harmonize them—to ensure that the pursuit of profit supports and amplifies the pursuit of purpose. Public health entrepreneurs who master this balance become formidable agents of change. They create businesses that are not only financially sustainable but also deeply impactful. They understand that purpose-driven profit is not a trade-off but a fusion that can transform lives and communities. Purpose and profit are not opposing forces but complementary allies. Together,

Purpose and Profit: Balancing Your Bottom Line with Your Higher Calling

they constitute the foundation of your entrepreneurial journey—a journey that leads to the intersection of purpose and profit and where your bottom line meets your higher calling.

Conclusion

Why the World Needs More Public Health Entrepreneurs

In most minds, public health and entrepreneurship are as opposite as it gets. One mental image conjures up stoic academics pouring over epidemiological data, the other an image of a spirited, out-of-the-box thinker, mover, and shaker. However, this seemingly dichotomous relationship is becoming increasingly blurred, and for good reason. "Entrepreneurs are individuals who recognize and act on opportunities to promote social change" (Storr, et al, 2022). And the public health sector, traditionally viewed as the keeper of the public's well-being, possesses an untapped potential to spark innovation, tackle global health crises, and drive sustainable impact by encouraging more entrepreneurs in the public health field. The missing link? The infusion of the entrepreneurial spirit, mindset, and skillset into public health initiatives is not just advantageous—but an urgent necessity.

The synergy between public health and entrepreneurship might not be immediately apparent; yet the need for this convergence has never been more critical. Public health issues — such as pandemics, chronic disease management, and health equity — present colossal challenges that require innovative solutions in healthcare delivery and the underlying systems and policies that support them. Storr et al. argue that entrepreneurs, especially commercial and social entrepreneurs, are necessary for communities to recover from pandemics because the recovery process of social crisis is dependent on experimentation, bottom-up discovery, and entrepreneurial action (2022).

We are in the midst of a profound paradigm shift, moving away from the traditional, siloed approach to healthcare, which primarily involves healthcare professionals. Instead, we are embracing a more inclusive model that actively involves public health professionals and engages the broader community. This evolving approach draws inspiration and insights from the entrepreneurial playbook, injecting new energy and creativity into the public health sector. As a result, we are witnessing the emergence of fresh perspectives, dynamic collaborations, and sustainable business models that hold the potential to drive meaningful change and address health challenges more effectively.

Academic Programs: Where are the Public Health Entrepreneur Programs?

Despite the growing recognition of entrepreneurial skills in public health, a notable gap persists in the educational landscape for future public health leaders. While fields like medicine, pharmacy, and law actively incorporate entrepreneurship into their curricula, public health education has been slower to adapt. This oversight warrants critical examination. Thankfully, some academic institutions are beginning to address this gap by introducing public health entrepreneurship courses. These programs serve as a vital bridge between theoretical knowledge and practical application. "Earning a living while addressing health and social issues is at the core of what many public health students seek to achieve from their education. Given their interests and the breadth of their training, public health students are uniquely positioned to act as practitioners, problem solvers, and potentially, public health entrepreneurs" (Hernandez et al., 2014).

Public health programs should include courses of study designed to expose students to the theory and practice of innovation in the public health setting because "entrepreneurship is both a mindset and a skillset. An entrepreneurship mindset cultivates the creative confidence to imagine solutions and the entrepreneurial skillset allows students to systematically test and iterate the steps and resources needed to build, launch, and implement their solutions" (Becket et al., 2019). By imparting both business acumen and a strong sense of social responsibility, these initiatives are shaping a new generation of public health professionals capable of driving impactful change within and beyond traditional healthcare environments.

A Blueprint for Public Health Entrepreneurship

Although entrepreneurship is most often associated with the pursuit of profit, the truth is that there are plenty of entrepreneurs who prioritize more than just financial gain. Public health and entrepreneurship, just like purpose and profit are not opposing forces but complementary allies. Not only does the world need both, the world should pursue both. So, how do we encourage the growth of public health entrepreneurship? It starts with a concerted effort to reframe public health not just as a social imperative but also as a business opportunity. We must foster environments that support risk-taking, innovation, and sustainable growth — the hallmarks of successful entrepreneurial ventures. Governments and international organizations can play critical roles in providing funding, mentorship, and regulatory support to public health entrepreneurs. Meanwhile, collaborative initiatives that bring together stakeholders from diverse sectors can create ecosystems where public health innovation can flourish. The burgeoning realm of public health entrepreneurship is bursting with promise, presenting an opportunity to embrace a profound shift in our approach to the public's health. We find ourselves on the cusp of a transformative era, where the conventional boundaries of public health are expanding, and entrepreneurs are leveraging their vision and drive to address humanity's most daunting health challenges.

For those already immersed in the field, I urge you to champion public health entrepreneurship within your spheres of influence. Collaborate with innovators, share resources generously, and strive for a future where public health and entrepreneurship are intricately intertwined.

For budding public health professionals, heed the call to action I have set before you. Equip yourselves with the tools of entrepreneurship, for you are the architects of a healthier, more prosperous world that we all strive to build.

And to the broader public, your support is paramount. Celebrate and invest in public health entrepreneurs who work tirelessly behind the scenes to uplift the public health profession, and champion health equity and a better quality of life for all. It is through collective action that we can unlock the full potential of public health entrepreneurship and pave the way for a brighter, healthier future for our world.

References

Becker, E. R. B., Chahine, T., & Shegog, R. (2019). Public Health Entrepreneurship: A Novel Path for Training Future Public Health Professionals. *Frontiers in public health*, 7, 89. https://doi.org/10.3389/fpubh.2019.00089.

Centers for Disease Control (2023, August 11). *Competencies for Public Health Professionals.* Public Health Professionals Gateway. Retrieved January 1, 2024, from https://www.cdc.gov/publichealthgateway/professional/competencies.html.

CDC Foundation (n.d.). What is Public Health? CDC Foundation. Retrieved January 1, 2024, from https://www.cdcfoundation.org/what-public-health.

Centers for Medicare and Medicaid Services (2023, September 28). *Health Equity.* CMS.gov. Retrieved January 1, 2024, from https://www.cms.gov/pillar/health-equity#:~:text=Health%20equity%20means%20the%20attainment,language%2C%20or%20other%20factors%20that.

Chahine T. (2021). Toward an Understanding of Public Health Entrepreneurship and Intrapreneurship. *Frontiers in public health*, 9, 593553. https://doi.org/10.3389/fpubh.2021.593553.

de Beaumont Foundation (October 2021). *Staffing Up Investing in the public health workforce.* Retrieved January 1, 2024, from https://debeaumont.org/staffing-up/.

de Beaumont Foundation (March 2022). *The impact of the COVID-10 pandemic: rising stress and burnout in public health.* Retrieved January 1, 2024, from https://debeaumont.org/phwins/2021-findings/stress-and-burnout/.

Golechha M. (2016). Health Promotion Methods for Smoking Prevention and Cessation: A Comprehensive Review of Effectiveness and the Way Forward. *International journal of preventive medicine, 7,* 7. https://doi.org/10.4103/2008-7802.173797.

Hernández, D., Carrión, D., Perotte, A., & Fullilove, R. (2014). Public health entrepreneurs: training the next generation of public health innovators. *Public health reports (Washington, D.C. : 1974), 129*(6), 477–481. https://doi.org/10.1177/003335491412900604.

Huang, T. T. K., Ciari, A., Costa, S. A., & Chahine, T. (2022). Advancing Public Health Entrepreneurship to Foster Innovation and Impact. *Frontiers in public health, 10*, 923764. https://doi.org/10.3389/fpubh.2022.923764.

Merid, M. W., Alem, A. Z., Chilot, D., Belay, D. G., Kibret, A. A., Asratie, M. H., Shibabaw, Y. Y., & Aragaw, F. M. (2023). Impact of access to improved water and sanitation on diarrhea reduction among rural under-five children in low and middle-income countries: a propensity score matched analysis. *Tropical medicine and health, 51*(1), 36. https://doi.org/10.1186/s41182-023-00525-9.

Ozawa, S., Clark, S., Portnoy, A., Grewal, S., Brenzel, L., & Walker, D. (2016). Return On Investment From Childhood Immunization In Low- And Middle-Income Countries. *Health Affairs, 35*(2), 199-207.

Rockwood, K. (2021, May 28). *The Hard Facts About Soft Skills: Why you should teach employees to be more resilient, communicative and creative.* SHRM.org. Retrieved January 1, 2024, from https://www.shrm.org/topics-tools/news/hr-magazine/hard-facts-soft-skills#:~:text=There%20are%20many%20ways%20a,a%20lack%20of%20soft%20skills.

Roman LA, Worthington K, Runnels L, Ilakkuvan, V. (2023). Describing the Self-Employed Public Health Consultant and Entrepreneur in the Workforce in the United States – Survey Findings and Practice Implications [Unpublished Manuscript]

Storr, V. H., Haeffele, S., Lofthouse, J. K., & Hobson, A. (2022). Entrepreneurship during a pandemic. *European journal of law and economics*, *54*(1), 83–105. https://doi.org/10.1007/s10657-021-09712-7.

World Health Organization (2018, February 22). *Health inequities and their causes*. Retrieved January 1, 2024, from https://www.who.int/news-room/facts-in-pictures/detail/health-inequities-and-their-causes.

Acknowledgments

Writing this book has been a journey filled with passion, perseverance, and the invaluable support of many individuals and organizations. I am deeply grateful to those who have contributed to the realization of this project and have played a vital role in its success.

First and foremost, I want to express my heartfelt gratitude to my #1 fans and my biggest supporters, my husband Chijioke, and my son, Xavier. Thank you for your unwavering encouragement and understanding throughout this book writing process and for your support of my business in general. Your belief in me and your endless support have been my pillars of strength.

I extend my sincere appreciation to my Co-Authors: Dr. Jovonni Spinner, Jometra Hawkins, and Vanessa Da Costa, my colleagues, who have shared their expertise, insights, and experiences generously. Your guidance has been instrumental in shaping the content of this book and our collective narrative that it is possible to make impact and income in the field of public health.

I am immensely thankful to Whitney Brooks at Empower Her Publishing, LLC for your professionalism, enthusiasm, and commitment to bringing this book to life. Your guidance in self-publishing made this process a breeze.

To the public health professionals and organizations who have inspired me with their innovative work and dedication to improving community health, your resilience and determination have illuminated the path toward a healthier future for all. I extend my admiration and gratitude. Your efforts serve as a continuous source of motivation and the reason that I love waking up every day to do this work.

Lastly, I want to express my appreciation to the readers (supporters) of this book. Your interest in public health entrepreneurship is a testament to the importance of this topic. I hope that the knowledge shared within these pages has empowered you to do great things in public health and in the world.

Thank you to all who have contributed to this project. Your support has been immeasurable and I am deeply grateful to each of you.

In service with heartfelt thanks,

Quisha

Bonus Content

PublicHealthPreneur™ Resources

As a token of my gratitude for your support of this book, I am delighted to offer you exclusive access to bonus content that will enrich your experience and deepen your insights gleaned from this book. To access more information on any of the resources below, go to quishaumemba.com/bookresources.

Extended Interviews
Dive deeper into the minds of the public health entrepreneurs featured in the book with extended video interviews. Gain additional perspectives, insider tips, and valuable insights that couldn't fit within the pages of the main text.

Interactive Worksheets
Put your newfound knowledge into action with interactive worksheets designed to help you apply key concepts to your own life and business. From goal-setting exercises to self-assessment tools, these worksheets will empower you to take tangible steps toward your business goals.

Exclusive Webinar
Get access to my free 90-minute webinar where I explore topics covered in the book in greater detail. Learn about the possibilities that exist in public health consulting and how to go from public health expert (or enthusiast) to public health entrepreneur.

Resource Library
Access a curated library of growing resources, including recommended readings, podcasts, courses of study, and tools to support your ongoing learning and growth beyond the pages of the book.

Free Resources
The Public Health Consultant's Starter Kit

A 44-page toolkit designed to help you start, grow, and scale a profitable public health consulting business.

The PublicHealthPreneur™ Podcast
A podcast where I share business tips, tactics, and strategies from my own experience to help you navigate the intersection of purpose and profit to make impact and income. Tune in on my YouTube channel or where you listen to your favorite podcasts.

The PublicHealthPreneur™ Blog
A blog where I share empowering stories, expert advice, practical resources, and the latest trends in public health consulting.

PublicHeathPrenurs™ Facebook Group
A Facebook group for current and aspiring #publichealthpreneurs who want to transform their passion for public health into profitable business ventures. While not a coaching community, the group is a space for shared learning, networking, and potential collaborations on impactful consulting projects.

Paid Offerings
PublicHealthPreneur™ Course
A completely self-paced course that teaches people how to start, grow, and scale a profitable public health consulting business and is based on my proprietary six-step system "Ready.Start.Launch!"

PublicHealthPreneur™ Academy
A group coaching program that provides public health consultants with tools, strategies, community, and expert guidance as they build and scale their consulting business. The coaching program features members-only events and challenges, plug-and-play downloadables, behind-the-scenes business tutorials, signature courses, live coaching sessions, and more.

Event Offerings
Ready.Set.Nework!
Ready.Set.Network! is the premiere networking event for public health professionals who are passionate about making a difference to connect, collaborate, exchange ideas with peers and build valuable connections that will help to elevate their career and/or business.

One-On-One Offerings
Quantum Leap VIP Day + Business Accelerator
Accelerate your results in an immersive high-impact VIP Day experience that garners rapid implementation and quick results. The VIP Day experience includes a 90-minute strategy session, a 4-hour intensive, and four weeks of coaching and accountability.

Clarity/Strategy Call
Allow me to take a deep dive into your specific business needs and provide a strategy that aligns with your expertise. This session results in a business roadmap, outlining the route from where you are to where you want to be.

Other Services
Speaking
Need a speaker that goes beyond the bullet points to deliver a memorable presentation? Book me! I am a dynamic presenter with a speaking style that is motivational, inspirational, and transformational, virtually or in-person. Speaking topics include business and entrepreneurship, healthcare/public health, or training and development.

Consulting
Let's explore how I can help you reach your goals. Whether your organization needs ongoing consulting or needs assistance with a specific project, drawing upon my background as a nurse and public health consultant, I offer a diverse skillset that covers a wide array of areas within the

healthcare and public health sectors. Let's collaborate and make a positive impact together!

Made in the USA
Middletown, DE
23 March 2024

51537654R00121